THE ASCENSION
Lenten
Companion

A Personal Encounter with the Power of the Gospel

YEAR A

Fr. Mark Toups

ASCENSION
West Chester, Pennsylvania

Ascension
Post Office Box 1990
West Chester, PA 19380
1-800-376-0520
ascensionpress.com

Cover art: Mike Moyers (*Follow Me* © 2023 Mike Moyers, Franklin, TN)
Interior art: Mike Moyers (*Temptation at the Pinnacle, Rise and Have No Fear, Conversation at the Well, Light of the World, Lazarus Come Out!, Hosanna!, Curtain Torn, Empty Tomb* © 2023 Mike Moyers, Franklin, TN)

Printed in the United States of America
ISBN 978-1-954881-50-1

CONTENTS

GETTING THE MOST OUT OF
THE ASCENSION LENTEN COMPANION

The book you have in your hands is the refreshed version of *The Ascension Lenten Companion* for Year A by Fr. Mark Toups. In response to feedback we received on its initial publication in 2020, we have made some changes. These changes align it with Years B and C of the series and include expanded meditations, new original artwork by Mike Moyers for each week, and the addition of the liturgical readings to the text itself.

This journal is meant to be used with a series of video presentations by Fr. Toups, which are freely available at **ascensionpress.com/lentencompanion**. We invite you to journey with him into the heart of the Lenten season this year.

Community

The *Lenten Companion* journal and videos are designed to be used by parishes, small groups, and individuals in preparation for Easter.

Community is a key component for growing in holiness. Lent provides a wonderful opportunity to take more time for prayer and grow stronger in friendship with others as you journey together to heaven.

The ideal is for a whole parish to take up and use the *Lenten Companion* together as a community. You can find out how to provide journals to a large parish group at **ascensionpress.com/lentencompanion**. You will find information there about obtaining bulk discounts and how to journey together using the *Lenten Companion* journal and videos.

If you are not able to experience the *Lenten Companion* as a whole parish, consider a small group setting. Use the *Lenten Companion* as a family devotion for Lent or get together with a few friends to talk about how God is speaking to you during this season. Bulk pricing is also available for small groups.

You can also take this journey through Lent even if you are not meeting in a group or talking about it with friends. The *Lenten Companion* is well suited to use as an individual. Remember that you are not alone—Catholics all over the country are on the same journey. This journal is a place for you to speak to God and hear and see all that he has to show you.

Videos

To accompany the journal, the *Lenten Companion* offers video presentations by Fr. Toups. Through his witness, spiritual direction, and prayer, you will find fresh insights into the profound love the Lord pours out for us in his Passion, Death, and Resurrection.

The seven video presentations are for Ash Wednesday, the five weeks of Lent, and Holy Week. The presentations are available on DVD and can also be viewed any time at **ascensionpress.com/lentencompanion**—where you can also sign up to get them sent to your inbox each week.

Daily Meditation and Prayer

The *Lenten Companion* is organized around the Sunday Gospel readings of Lent Cycle A. Each day, a new meditation invites you to draw closer to Jesus as you accompany him through the Gospel events.

You will notice that the meditations are grouped by week and that each week starts on a Thursday. This puts the Sunday Gospel reading right at the center of the week's meditations. The meditations from Thursday through Saturday help you prepare your heart for the Gospel you will hear proclaimed at Mass on Sunday, and the remaining meditations, through the following Wednesday, further unpack the same Gospel reading.

Each meditation is followed by a spiritual exercise titled "For Your Prayer." Throughout the Lenten season, this section asks you to reflect on the Sunday Gospel or a related passage and invites you to encounter the Lord in his love as you pray. Some of these spiritual exercises are intentionally repeated to encourage you to venture more deeply into prayer. The time you spend in prayer with the Lord is the true heart of the *Lenten Companion*.

Praying with Scripture

Many people find it helpful to follow these steps when praying with Scripture and Scripture-based scenes: (1) prepare, (2) acknowledge, (3) relate, (4) receive, and (5) respond.

Prepare

When you are praying with Scripture, open your Bible and read the passage once. If you are praying imaginatively, read through the scene. Get familiar with the words. Then slowly read the text a second time.

Pay attention to how you feel as you read. Pay attention to which words strike you. When the text sets a scene, enter the scene with the people mentioned in it. Once the passage or the scene comes to its natural conclusion, continue with ARRR.

ARRR

ARRR stands for **acknowledge, relate, receive, and respond**.

You have sat with God's Word. You have entered the scene. Now, when you feel that God is saying something to you, *acknowledge what stirs within you.* Pay attention to your thoughts, feelings, and desires. These are important.

After acknowledging what's going on in your heart, *relate that to God.* Don't just think about your thoughts, feelings, and desires. Don't just think about God or how God might react. Relate to God. Tell him how you feel. Tell him what you think. Tell him what you want. Share all your thoughts, feelings, and desires with God. Share everything with him.

Once you have shared everything with God, *receive from him.* Listen to what he is telling you. It could be a subtle voice you hear. It could be a memory that pops up. Maybe he invites you to reread the Scripture passage. Maybe he invites you into a still, restful silence. Trust that God is listening to you, and receive what he wants to share with you.

Now *respond to him.* Your response could be to continue your conversation with God. It could be resolving to do something. It could be tears or laughter. Respond to what you're receiving.

Journal

The last step is to journal. Keep a record of your prayer this Lent. Your journal entry does not have to be lengthy. It could be a single word or a sentence or two about what God told you or how the day's reflection struck you. However you do it, journaling will help you walk closer to God this Lent. We have provided journaling space for you each day.

Commit

As you dedicate yourself to prayer this Lent, there is no better safeguard than a good plan. We recommend the five Ws as a method of prayer planning. Here is how it works. Every Sunday, look at your calendar and write out your plan for the next six days, answering the following questions: When? Where? What? Who? and Why?

WHEN will I spend time with Jesus?

WHERE will I spend time with Jesus?

WHAT are Jesus and I going to do together?

WHO will hold me accountable for my time with Jesus?

WHY am I prioritizing my time with Jesus?

Making a commitment is the first step in transforming your prayer life. These weeks with *The Ascension Lenten Companion, Year A* are the perfect time to begin.

Introduction

The Church gives us Lent as a time of personal renewal and spiritual growth. But for many Catholics, the experience of Lent is compromised from the very beginning. Far too often, we make our experience of Lent more about us than about Jesus. In other words, we make it about what we are giving up rather than deepening our relationship with the Lord.

Every Ash Wednesday, we hear these words from the prophet Joel: "Rend your hearts, not your garments, and return to the LORD, your God" (Joel 2:13). God wants our hearts more than anything else. The purpose of Lenten penance is to dispose us to a more vibrant relationship with God, a more generous self-gift to others, and a more open receptivity to God's will. It is in the dynamics of an authentic relationship that we experience personal renewal and spiritual growth. Lent, then, can be a season of transformation.

To rend is to tear or split. This Lent, we will rend our hearts by praying into and through each Sunday's Gospel reading. Every Thursday, we will begin preparing for the Gospel that we will hear proclaimed at Mass on Sunday, and we will unpack it further the following Monday through Wednesday. This will help us deepen our experience of each Sunday of Lent.

I am praying for you as you seek out the Lord and open yourself to a new experience of his love.

Welcome to Lent. Welcome to the journey.

Heart

"Rend your hearts, not your garments,
and return to the Lord, your God."

– JOEL 2:13

Ash Wednesday

"What are you doing for Lent?" Many are asking this question. Perhaps you are asking this question. Experience teaches us that most of us will do this year what we did last year, and most did last year what they did in years past. However, there is a saying, "If you do what you have always done, you will get what you always got." Perhaps this is why you are reading this book. Perhaps you want more from God. Perhaps you want this Lent to be different. If this is true, welcome. This is going to be a great Lent.

Many of us are familiar with the phrase *Lenten sacrifice*. When we hear the word "sacrifice," most of us think about giving up something. Many do give up something during Lent. However, the word "sacrifice" has less to do with giving something *up* than with giving something *to*. "Sacrifice" is derived from the Latin *sacra* and *facere,* which together mean "to make holy." Sacrifice is more about *what we offer* than about what we give up.

Adopting a Lenten sacrifice as a spiritual exercise is a good thing. However, if we stay true to the real meaning of the word, we need to go a bit deeper. So the question for you is this: What can you offer to God? Instead of giving something up, can you give something to the Lord? What about your heart? What if you offered your heart to God this Lent?

Listen to the words of the *Catechism of the Catholic Church*: "If our heart is far from God, the words of prayer are in vain" (CCC 2562). This Lent, God wants you. God wants your heart. What God really wants from you is *you*. God wants your time, your dreams, your concerns, and everything in your heart. He wants your fear, your sin, your shame, your addictions, and your weakness. He wants everything in your heart. He wants the good, the bad, and the ugly. God is not afraid of anything that is in your heart. If you want this Lent to be different, then where you start has to be different. The place to start is your heart.

Here's the good news: At the end of Lent, God is going to give himself completely to you as the perfect sacrifice on the Cross. God is going to give you everything. God is not going to withhold anything from you. He is going to give you and the entire world his body. He is going to give us his entire heart.

For Your Prayer

Read Psalm 63:1–9. Read it three times very slowly. Then rewrite the verses in your own words.

Offer God everything in your heart.

What words stood out to you as you prayed?
What did you find stirring in your heart?

_____

_____

_____

_____

_____

_____

_____

_____

_____

_____

_____

_____

_____

_____

_____

_____

_____

_____

_____

_____

_____

_____

The Temptation
in the Desert

FIRST READING

GENESIS 2:7–9; 3:1–7

The LORD God formed man out of the clay of the ground and blew into his nostrils the breath of life, and so man became a living being. Then the LORD God planted a garden in Eden, in the east, and placed there the man whom he had formed. Out of the ground the LORD God made various trees grow that were delightful to look at and good for food, with the tree of life in the middle of the garden and the tree of the knowledge of good and evil.

Now the serpent was the most cunning of all the animals that the LORD God had made. The serpent asked the woman, "Did God really tell you not to eat from any of the trees in the garden?" The woman answered the serpent: "We may eat of the fruit of the trees in the garden; it is only about the fruit of the tree in the middle of the garden that God said, 'You shall not eat it or even touch it, lest you die.'" But the serpent said to the woman: "You certainly will not die! No, God knows well that the moment you eat of it your eyes will be opened and you will be like gods who know what is good and what is evil." The woman saw that the tree was good for food, pleasing to the eyes, and desirable for gaining wisdom. So she took some of its fruit and ate it; and she also gave some to her husband, who was with her, and he ate it.

Then the eyes of both of them were opened, and they realized that they were naked; so they sewed fig leaves together and made loincloths for themselves.

RESPONSORIAL PSALM

Psalm 51:3–4, 5–6, 12–13, 17

R. Be merciful, O Lord, for we have sinned.

Have mercy on me, O God, in your goodness;
    in the greatness of your compassion wipe out my offense.
Thoroughly wash me from my guilt
    and of my sin cleanse me.

For I acknowledge my offense,
    and my sin is before me always:
"Against you only have I sinned,
    and done what is evil in your sight."

A clean heart create for me, O God,
    and a steadfast spirit renew within me.
Cast me not out from your presence,
    and your Holy Spirit take not from me.

Give me back the joy of your salvation,
    and a willing spirit sustain in me.
O Lord, open my lips,
    and my mouth shall proclaim your praise.

SECOND READING

Romans 5:12, 17–19

Brothers and sisters: Through one man sin entered the world, and through sin, death, and thus death came to all men, inasmuch as all sinned.

For if, by the transgression of the one, death came to reign through that one, how much more will those who receive the abundance of grace and of the gift of justification come to reign in life through the one Jesus Christ.

In conclusion, just as through one transgression condemnation came upon all, so, through one righteous act, acquittal and life came to all. For just as through the disobedience of the one man the many were made sinners, so, through the obedience of the one, the many will be made righteous.

GOSPEL

Matthew 4:1–11

At that time Jesus was led by the Spirit into the desert to be tempted by the devil. He fasted for forty days and forty nights, and afterwards he was hungry. The tempter approached and said to him, "If you are the Son of God, command that these stones become loaves of bread."

He said in reply, "It is written: *One does not live on bread alone, but on every word that comes forth from the mouth of God.*"

Then the devil took him to the holy city, and made him stand on the parapet of the temple, and said to him, "If you are the Son of God, throw yourself down. For it is written: *He will command his angels concerning you and with their hands they will support you, lest you dash your foot against a stone.*" Jesus answered him, "Again it is written, *You shall not put the Lord, your God, to the test.*"

Then the devil took him up to a very high mountain, and showed him all the kingdoms of the world in their magnificence, and he said to him, "All these I shall give to you, if you will prostrate yourself and worship me." At this, Jesus said to him, "Get away, Satan! It is written: *The Lord, your God, shall you worship and him alone shall you serve.*"

Then the devil left him and, behold, angels came and ministered to him.

Led

"Jesus was led by the Spirit into the desert to be tempted by the devil."

– MATTHEW 4:1

Today we look forward to the Gospel for the First Sunday of Lent. There is a strategic temptation that confronts most of us in the early days of Lent, a temptation that subtly puts too much focus on *us*. Let us be clear at the very beginning of this journey: Lent is not about you.

Lent is not about how we are doing a day after ashes, nor is it about whether we can keep our Lenten sacrifices until Easter. Lent isn't about our pursuit of self-perfection or what we can do over the next forty days. Lent is not about what we are doing as much as it is about what God is doing. In fact, the reason most of us struggle with prayer is because, if we are honest, most of us live self-absorbed lives, and we can only handle so much introspection before we get bored with it.

Pope Benedict XVI, in his encyclical *Deus Caritas Est* ("God Is Love"), writes, "Being Christian is not the result of an ethical choice or a lofty idea, but the encounter with an event, a person, which gives life a new horizon and a decisive direction."[1] Being Christian is not about choosing Jesus; it is about Jesus choosing us. Being Christian is, in its essence, about a person in a personal relationship with Jesus Christ. Lent is not about the externals. It is about an encounter with the person of Jesus Christ.

Jesus is the one who wants this Lent to be a transformational time in your life. Jesus is the one who wants you to give your heart to him. Jesus is the one taking the initiative in your life. Therefore, if you are going to encounter Jesus, then you must let him lead you. You must ask for the grace to be led.

Jesus wants to lead you because Jesus himself knows what it is like to be led. At every moment of his life Jesus was led by the

Father. In the same way, Jesus is trying to lead you. Many of us resist being led by God, either because we do not believe that God is really involved in our daily lives or because we are afraid of where he might lead us.

Today, we begin to look ahead to the Gospel that we will encounter in just a few days on the first Sunday of Lent. There, in Matthew 4:1, we will read how Jesus "was led by the Spirit into the desert to be tempted by the devil." We will learn that Jesus was led to face temptation. However, here is the key point about Jesus being led: Jesus trusted where he was being led because he trusted who was leading him. He trusted God. The same is true for us: when you struggle to let God lead you, stop focusing on where he is leading you and refocus on him, on the One who is leading you.

For Your Prayer

Read Matthew 4:1–11. Read it three times very slowly. What word or phrase tugs at your heart? Talk to God about how this word or phrase applies to your life.

What words stood out to you as you prayed?
What did you find stirring in your heart?

_____
_____
_____
_____
_____
_____
_____
_____
_____
_____
_____
_____
_____
_____
_____
_____
_____
_____
_____
_____
_____
_____
_____

Intentional

"He fasted for forty days and forty nights."

– MATTHEW 4:2

Friday after
Ash Wednesday

In Matthew 4:2 we read that Jesus "fasted for forty days and forty nights." Why forty? As Pope Benedict XVI writes in his book *Jesus of Nazareth*, "In Jesus' day the number forty was already filled with rich symbolism for Israel. First of all, it recalls Israel's forty years' wandering in the desert, a period in which the people were both tempted and enjoyed a special closeness to God. The forty days and nights also remind us of the forty days that Moses spent on Mount Sinai before he was privileged to receive the word of God, the sacred tablets of the Covenant."[2]

Yesterday, we learned that Jesus was led to the desert. He was led there intentionally. The Father wanted to bless his Son and therefore led him into the desert. Likewise, God is leading you into the desert of Lent for forty days so you may grow spiritually.

The fact that Jesus is led to the desert intentionally is important for us. Rarely do we grow unless we are intentional about our growth. Intentionality primarily requires three things: we have to know what we want, we have to have a plan, and we have to have people hold us accountable. So I ask you at the beginning of this Lenten journey: What do you want God to do in your life? When are you going to carve out time for prayer? Who is going to hold you accountable? Lent can be life-changing, but it will not just happen; you must be intentional.

Second, intentionality requires that we have the courage to ask ourselves what may be preventing our spiritual growth. In other words, if we are going to carve out time for prayer, we may have to let go of using our time for other things. It is not that we do not have enough time, but that we do not use our time well. If we are going to be intentional about growing spiritually, we must be intentional about not doing the things that prevent us from growth.

Third, intentionality requires depth. If we are going to ask people to hold us accountable, then we have to have the courage to have a conversation with them at a very particular depth. This may require a bit more vulnerability as we share why we are asking them to hold us accountable. This will also mean that the conversation shifts to a deeper level, from the more superficial things of life to the more substantial things.

This Lent can be a powerful experience of the Lord. To receive this experience, we must remain intentional.

For Your Prayer

Again today, as you did yesterday, read Matthew 4:1–11. Read it three times very slowly. Which word or phrase tugs at your heart today? Talk to God about how this word or phrase applies to your life.

What words stood out to you as you prayed?
What did you find stirring in your heart?

Weakness

"He fasted for forty days and forty nights, and afterwards he was hungry. The tempter approached and said to him, 'If you are the Son of God, command that these stones become loaves of bread.'"

– MATTHEW 4:2–3

After forty days of fasting, Jesus is hungry. Recalling what we learned yesterday, it is important to remember that Jesus has been led into the desert intentionally. Thus, when Jesus experiences profound physical hunger, there is something intentional that the Father is attempting to accomplish. Jesus is hungry. Jesus is weak. It is precisely here, in his weakness, that the first temptation strikes. Jesus is tempted in his hunger. Jesus is tempted in his weakness.

You and I can learn much from this, for each of us has our own greatest weakness. This weakness, the weakness we speak of today, is not that of a physical nature. St. Ignatius of Loyola teaches that the enemy "conducts himself as a leader, intent upon conquering and robbing what he desires. For, just as a captain and leader of an army in the field, pitching his camp and exploring the fortifications and defenses of a stronghold, attacks it at the weakest point, in the same way the enemy of human nature, roving about, looks in turn at all our theological, cardinal, and moral virtues; and where he finds us weakest and most in need for our eternal salvation, there he attacks us and attempts to take us."[3]

We all have our own greatest moral weakness. We all have a place where we are most susceptible to temptation. Therefore, it is important for us to know the reality of our hearts.

Let's recap where we have been these first few days. God wants our hearts. For some of us, it can be uncomfortable to peer into our hearts and be honest about what is there. God uses seasons like Lent to lead us so that we can grow. If we are going to let God lead us, we must be honest about what is in our hearts. That means being honest with God about our weakness.

Two people know of Jesus' weakness. Of course, we see the tempter speaking to Jesus about his weakness. But notice how Jesus, in quoting Scripture, keeps his focus on his relationship with the Father. When the tempter speaks to us about our weakness, his words are always filled with accusation and temptation. When God speaks to us about our weakness, his words are filled with hope and his longing for us. The Father knows Jesus is hungry and soon provides for him.

God knows your weakness and longs to be with you there. Be not afraid, for God loves you. In fact, he loves you most in your weakness.

For Your Prayer

Read Psalm 139:1–16. Read it three times very slowly. What word or phrase tugs at your heart? Talk to God about how this word or phrase applies to your life.

What words stood out to you as you prayed?
What did you find stirring in your heart?

_____

_____

_____

_____

_____

_____

_____

_____

_____

_____

_____

_____

_____

_____

_____

_____

_____

_____

_____

_____

Immediately

"[Jesus] said in reply, 'It is written: One does not live on bread alone, but on every word that comes forth from the mouth of God.'"

– MATTHEW 4:4

Sunday of the First Week of Lent

Notice how quickly Jesus responds to the temptation: he responds immediately. Jesus responds boldly to the temptation because he knows the voice of the tempter; he is aware of the one who is speaking to him.

Returning to St. Ignatius of Loyola and his *Spiritual Exercises*, we learn more about the nature of temptation and the need to respond immediately. In his twelfth rule for the discernment of spirits, St. Ignatius points out that the enemy is weak when faced with strength and strong when faced with weakness.[4] So at the very first hint of temptation, we must act immediately. We must avoid negotiating with temptation. Whenever we engage with a temptation, we engage with the tempter. Every temptation is a disguised attempt to lure us away from God and toward the enemy.

When we are tempted to sin, we must act boldly and immediately to reject it. If we say no immediately, the temptation—the tempter—flees immediately. But if we flirt with the temptation, we flirt with the tempter. The temptation builds strength and becomes more appealing. Attempting to say no to temptation after we have entertained it often leads to failure.

If a snowball starts to roll down a mountain, when do you want to stop it? If you stop it at the top of the mountain, it remains just a snowball. But if you let it keep rolling, it gains momentum and size. Quickly it becomes a boulder, and if you try to stop it then, you may get hurt. If it triggers an avalanche, others will be hurt too. The same is true of temptation: We must stop temptation at the top of the mountain. We must act immediately.

For Your Prayer

Read James 4:7–12. Read verse 7 three times very slowly. What is God saying to you about temptation? What is your typical response to temptation?

What words stood out to you as you prayed?
What did you find stirring in your heart?

_____

_____

_____

_____

_____

_____

_____

_____

_____

_____

_____

_____

_____

_____

_____

_____

Lie

"[The devil] said to him, 'If you are the Son of God, throw yourself down. For it is written: He will command his angels concerning you and with their hands they will support you, lest you dash your foot against a stone.'"

– MATTHEW 4:6

Y ou've probably heard it said that the enemy cloaks his lies in 90 percent truth. Temptations are saying something to us, and many times 90 percent of the statement is true. But 10 percent is a lie.

Let me give you an example. My greatest weakness centers on doing things well. There is a particular vulnerability within my heart around feeling that I am failing. When I fail or when I feel like a failure, I am affected emotionally and spiritually, and I am confronted by my weakness. There, in that place of weakness and vulnerability, I often hear a whisper from the enemy that sounds something like this: "You failed. You know you failed. God knows you failed. God sees what you did and why you did it. You're alone."

Let's unpack that temptation and see how the enemy has enclosed his lie in a statement that is 90 percent true. Assume that I heard the whisper from the enemy after I had failed at something. In the whisper, the phrase "you failed" is true. I did fail. Likewise, the statement "you know you failed" is also true. Furthermore, the statement "God knows you failed" is true. Continuing, the statement that "God sees what you did and why you did it" is true. So far everything that the enemy has said to me is true. But notice the strategic seduction in the final piece of the temptation: "You're alone." While everything preceding those two words is true, the final two words of the temptation are completely false. That's how the enemy has enclosed his lie in a temptation that is 90 percent true. It's because the first 90 percent is true that we believe that the lie has weight.

Matthew 4:6 reveals such a temptation as Satan tempts Jesus to prove that he is the Son of God. Would the angels be there if Jesus threw himself down? Yes. Would Jesus be held up by them? Yes. So far, Satan's assertions to Jesus are true. Notice, though, the deception at the very beginning of the temptation: "If you are the Son of God." What this short clause suggests is 100 percent false. Jesus is the Son of God. Proving it—or not proving it—does not change the fact that Jesus is who he says he is. The enemy has cloaked the lie in the truth.

Think about your most alluring temptation. What is it offering you? Temptation never provides what it promises. Never. Ever. Tucked inside every temptation is a lie.

For Your Prayer

Read 1 John 4:1–6. Read it three times very slowly.
Today, with Jesus, look at your most alluring temptation.
What is it offering you? How is it lying to you?

What words stood out to you as you prayed?
What did you find stirring in your heart?

Resist

"Jesus answered him, 'Again it is written, You
shall not put the Lord, your God, to the test.'"

– MATTHEW 4:7

In Matthew 4:5–6, we read, "Then the devil took him to the holy city, and made him stand on the parapet of the temple, and said to him, 'If you are the Son of God, throw yourself down. For it is written: *He will command his angels concerning you and with their hands they will support you, lest you dash your foot against a stone.*'"

Jesus immediately responds to the second temptation: "You shall not put the Lord, your God, to the test." Here Jesus is quoting Deuteronomy 6:16, which clearly indicates that we should not test God. However, it is important to notice too that the commandment in Deuteronomy 6:16 was given when Israel had been struggling for forty years in the desert. This struggle was intentional; it had a purpose. God was forming his people and teaching them to trust him. God was intentionally leading Israel through the desert, and he was with them when they were tested.

In his *Spiritual Exercises*, St. Ignatius of Loyola speaks of experiences when we might not hear God or see or feel him. Ignatius calls this *spiritual desolation*. He describes spiritual desolation as "darkness of soul, disturbance in it, movement to low and earthly things, disquiet from various agitations and temptations, moving to lack of confidence, without hope, without love, finding oneself totally slothful, tepid, sad and as if separated from one's Creator and Lord."[5]

He is describing a situation in which you and I will experience temptation. He then says, "Let one who is in desolation consider how ... he may resist the various agitations and temptations of the enemy; since he can resist with the divine help, which always remains with him, though he does not clearly feel it."[6]

Why does God allow temptation? We could write a whole book just on that question. One reason God allows temptation is to teach us how to resist. Let me explain.

Muscles grow stronger only with resistance. Likewise, there is something about learning how to resist that makes us stronger in our spiritual lives.

For Your Prayer

Read James 1:12–27. Read it three times very slowly. Today, with Jesus, look at your most alluring temptation. What is God trying to teach you? How is God trying to teach you to resist?

What words stood out to you as you prayed?
What did you find stirring in your heart?

_____

_____

_____

_____

_____

_____

_____

_____

_____

_____

_____

_____

_____

_____

_____

_____

_____

_____

_____

_____

_____

_____

Easy

*"And he said to him, 'All these I shall give to you, if
you will prostrate yourself and worship me.'"*

– MATTHEW 4:9

In the third temptation, the tempter offers Jesus all the kingdoms of the world: "All these I shall give to you, if you will prostrate yourself and worship me." What specifically is the temptation here?

Let's start with Jesus' relationship with the Father. Jesus perfectly receives all that the Father will give him. In the Gospel of John, Jesus says, "Amen, amen, I say to you, a son cannot do anything on his own, but only what he sees his father doing; for what he does, his son will do also. For the Father loves his Son and shows him everything that he himself does, and he will show him greater works than these, so that you may be amazed" (John 5:19–20, NAB). In a sense Jesus is saying, "I only do what the Father tells me to do. I only say what the Father tells me to say. The Father gives me everything."

Living in unbridled obedience to the Father is precisely what safeguards Jesus' communion with the Father. However, this obedience doesn't mean that life is easy. Jesus will endure his crowning with thorns. He will be beaten and scourged. The suffering of Jesus' Passion will fulfill Isaiah's prophecies of the Suffering Servant.

Therefore, in a sense, the third temptation is offering Jesus what is already his but without the suffering. The enemy is saying, "I'll give it to you. You won't have to suffer. I'll make it easy."

If we are honest, most of us want things easy, especially when it comes to our relationship with God. Most of us do not like to struggle. Most of us run from suffering. When it comes to the things that are deeply personal, when it comes to the things of our interior life, many of us want it to be easy.

How many of us resist, run away from, or do not even believe in suffering as part of our spiritual life? In fact, there is probably something about your most alluring temptation that either promises to make life easier or alleviate suffering. But life is not easy. Suffering is a part of life.

Here is the key: Either I am experiencing God with me in my suffering or I am enduring the suffering alone. I often quote my friend Charles Mack, who once said to me, "Life is a lot less about what you're facing and a lot more about where you're looking."

No matter what we are facing in our spiritual life, we are always looking at the Lord. When we are with God in our suffering, his strength becomes our strength. But when I think I am enduring the suffering alone, I instinctively grasp at something to make it easier. Jesus knows that his life will not be easy. And he will atone for the sins of humanity, many of which were sins that promised to make life easy.

For Your Prayer

Read Hebrews 12:1–13. Read it three times very slowly. What word or phrase tugs at your heart? Talk to God about how this word or phrase applies to your life.

What words stood out to you as you prayed?
What did you find stirring in your heart?

_____

_____

_____

_____

_____

_____

_____

_____

_____

_____

_____

_____

_____

_____

_____

_____

_____

_____

_____

_____

_____

_____

Take a moment to reflect on the past week, going over the meditations that bore the most fruit in your prayer, the things you wrote, and your reflections from the video.

The Transfiguration

FIRST READING

GENESIS 12:1–4A

The LORD said to Abram: "Go forth from the land of your kinsfolk and from your father's house to a land that I will show you.

"I will make of you a great nation, and I will bless you; I will make your name great, so that you will be a blessing. I will bless those who bless you and curse those who curse you. All the communities of the earth shall find blessing in you."

Abram went as the LORD directed him.

RESPONSORIAL PSALM

PSALM 33:4–5, 18–19, 20, 22

R. Lord, let your mercy be on us, as we place our trust in you.

Upright is the word of the LORD,
    and all his works are trustworthy.
He loves justice and right;
    of the kindness of the LORD the earth is full.

See, the eyes of the LORD are upon those who fear him,
    upon those who hope for his kindness,
To deliver them from death
    and preserve them in spite of famine.

Our soul waits for the LORD,
    who is our help and our shield.
May your kindness, O LORD, be upon us
    who have put our hope in you.

SECOND READING

2 Timothy 1:8b–10

Beloved: Bear your share of hardship for the gospel with the strength that comes from God.

He saved us and called us to a holy life, not according to our works but according to his own design and the grace bestowed on us in Christ Jesus before time began, but now made manifest through the appearance of our savior Christ Jesus, who destroyed death and brought life and immortality to light through the gospel.

GOSPEL

Matthew 17:1–9

Jesus took Peter, James, and John his brother, and led them up a high mountain by themselves. And he was transfigured before them; his face shone like the sun and his clothes became white as light. And behold, Moses and Elijah appeared to them, conversing with him. Then Peter said to Jesus in reply, "Lord, it is good that we are here. If you wish, I will make three tents here, one for you, one for Moses, and one for Elijah."

While he was still speaking, behold, a bright cloud cast a shadow over them, then from the cloud came a voice that said, "This is my beloved Son, with whom I am well pleased; listen to him."

When the disciples heard this, they fell prostrate and were very much afraid. But Jesus came and touched them, saying, "Rise, and do not be afraid." And when the disciples raised their eyes, they saw no one else but Jesus alone.

As they were coming down from the mountain, Jesus charged them, "Do not tell the vision to anyone until the Son of Man has been raised from the dead."

Mountain

"Jesus took Peter, James, and John his brother, and led them up a high mountain by themselves."

– MATTHEW 17:1

Today, our attention shifts as we transition from the Gospel for the First Sunday of Lent and prepare for the Gospel of the Second Sunday of Lent. While we remain in the Gospel of Matthew, we shift from chapter 4 to chapter 17. Here we read of the account of the Transfiguration.

The Transfiguration happens atop Mount Tabor. Why is this significant? In the Bible, mountains are an significant image. God uses mountains to reveal himself to his people. It was on Mount Ararat that Noah's ark came to rest after the Flood. It was on Mount Moriah that God forged ahead with Abraham as he was tempted with Isaac. It was on Mount Sinai that God revealed himself to Moses, giving him the Ten Commandments and bestowing upon him the covenant.

Biblically, mountains are seen as holy. Mountains are often the place where God appears. So when Jesus takes Peter, James, and John to the top of a mountain, we expect something to happen because of where they are going.

In each mountain experience in the Bible, God reveals himself to people. This is important. God wants to be known; God wants to reveal himself to us. Of course, sometimes it is difficult for us to find God—because life isn't easy or we fail to resist temptation or we believe the lies of the enemy. The ultimate temptation is to believe that God is not here, that he cannot be found.

Let me share a bit of my heart with you in a personal example. A few days ago I shared that fear of failure is perhaps my strongest temptation. I mentioned that the temptation centers on being abandoned. The fear is that because I have failed, I myself am a failure. Furthermore, the temptation says to me that because

I am a failure, God is disappointed in me and no longer wants to be with me. Thus, because I have failed, I have forced God to leave me, and I am now alone.

The account of the Transfiguration can occasionally feel like an experience in Jesus' life that is disconnected from our lives. But what God is revealing in the Transfiguration is very personal for us. God wants to be known. God wants to reveal himself. We are never alone, for God is forever reaching out to us.

Be not afraid. We will come to see how the Transfiguration has much to teach us. God wants to reveal himself to you in your temptations, in your struggles, in your suffering. He is there, revealing himself to you there.

For Your Prayer

Read Matthew 17:1–9. Read it three times, very slowly. What word or phrase tugs at your heart? Talk to God about how this word or phrase applies to your life.

What words stood out to you as you prayed?
What did you find stirring in your heart?

_____

_____

_____

_____

_____

_____

_____

_____

_____

_____

_____

_____

_____

_____

_____

_____

_____

_____

_____

_____

_____

_____

Transfigured

*"And he was transfigured before them; his face shone
like the sun and his clothes became white as light."*

– MATTHEW 17:2

Yesterday we learned that mountains are places where God reveals himself. The next logical question that we might ask is this: what specifically is God revealing to us in the event of the Transfiguration?

In the Transfiguration, God is revealing that Jesus is the Christ, the Son of God. In being transfigured before them, Jesus is giving the Apostles a glimpse of his heavenly glory that is hidden in the human appearance of his flesh. The Transfiguration opens the minds of the Apostles and shows them that Jesus is who he says he is. Jesus is the Messiah. Jesus is God. As God, Jesus has the victory over all things.

There was a particular season in my past when I was struggling. I was struggling so much that I doubted that God was with me. I remember praying one day and saying something like "God, please help me if you can." Soon, I was stunned as I heard back from God in my heart as he said, "If I can? Who do you think you are talking to?" As soon as I heard these words, there was a profound moment of sober silence. I knew that it was the voice of the Lord. After a few more moments of intentional stillness and listening, I heard him speak further: "Do you believe I am who I say I am? Do you believe I do what I promise to do?"

I felt as if the questions were so important that I needed to give a reverential and sacred answer. I knew that I had to actually consider the reality of the question if there was going to be integrity in my response.

Do I really believe that God is who he says he is? Jesus never claims to be a good teacher or a nice guy. None of the modern claims about Jesus match the claims that Jesus himself makes.

Jesus claims to be one thing and one thing only: Jesus claims to be God in the flesh. I was confronted that day with the question that every Christian must allow themselves to confront. It's irrelevant to ask myself who I believe Jesus to be. The question is irrelevant. The only question that matters is, Do I believe that Jesus is who he says he is? That's the only question.

As I continued to consider the question that day, I came to feel deep peace and profound trust. I knew the voice of the one who was speaking to me. And in that moment, I fully understood that he is who he says he is.

Today, ask Jesus what he is trying to do in your life this Lent. Ask him where he is proving to you that he is who he says he is.

For Your Prayer

Read Romans 8:18–39. Read it three times very slowly. What word or phrase tugs at your heart? Talk to God about how this word or phrase applies to your life.

What words stood out to you as you prayed?
What did you find stirring in your heart?

Face

*"And behold, Moses and Elijah appeared
to them, conversing with him."*

– MATTHEW 17:3

In the Transfiguration, God's glory is made visible. This coincides with the appearance of Moses and Elijah. Why Moses and Elijah?

In Exodus, Moses stands atop Mount Sinai and wants to see God's glory. God does reveal himself to Moses, but Moses must hide so that he sees only the back of the Lord as the Lord passes by. "You cannot see my face," says the Lord, "for no one can see me and live" (Exodus 33:20, NAB). Moses wanted to see the face of God but was not able to do so.

Moses is not alone. The other Old Testament figure who experiences God's glory on a mountain is Elijah. In 1 Kings 19, Elijah is also atop Mount Sinai. The Lord reveals himself there to Elijah in "a light silent sound." But Elijah knows it is the Lord and hides his face in his cloak, as if he also knows that he cannot see God's face and live (see 1 Kings 19:9-3, NAB).

Atop Mount Tabor, Jesus has brought with him Peter, James, and John. When the Apostles witness the Transfiguration, they also see Moses and Elijah with the Lord. Now these two men, Moses and Elijah, see God's face in the face of Jesus. God is not invisible.

There is something powerful about the fact that God has a human face. With a face, God has eyes. Jesus sees us—and we are seen from his perspective, not ours. With a face, God has ears. Jesus hears everything, even the deepest longings beyond words. With a face, God has a voice. Jesus speaks to us in the silence, a silence that for many people is most difficult to find these days.

Jesus wants you to know him. God is not invisible. He wants to be known and seen and heard.

The *Catechism* teaches us that "God calls man first. Man may forget his Creator or hide far from his face; he may run after idols or accuse the deity of having abandoned him; yet the living and true God tirelessly calls each person to that mysterious encounter known as prayer. In prayer, the faithful God's initiative of love always comes first; our own first step is always a response" (CCC 2567).

The Church teaches us that God is the one who is taking the initiative. God is the one who is calling us first. God is the one who is reaching out to us. Regardless of how fainthearted our pursuit of God has been, God is forever desiring for us to see him, to hear him, and to know him.

For Your Prayer

Read Jeremiah 29:11–14. Read it three times very slowly. What word or phrase tugs at your heart? Talk to God about how this word or phrase applies to your life.

What words stood out to you as you prayed?
What did you find stirring in your heart?

Identity

"While he was still speaking, behold, a bright cloud cast a shadow over them, then from the cloud came a voice that said, 'This is my beloved Son, with whom I am well pleased; listen to him.'"

– MATTHEW 17:5

Sunday of the Second Week of Lent

Today at Mass we hear the the Gospel for the Sunday of the Second Week of Lent proclaimed— namely, the Transfiguration. The Father speaks during the Transfiguration, saying, "This is my beloved Son." Three words capture everything for Jesus. Three words define the entirety of Jesus' identity. Three words: "my beloved Son."

The entirety of Jesus is defined by the Father. Jesus' identity is bestowed on him in his conception, revealed in his baptism, and confirmed in the Transfiguration. He knows who he is because he knows whose he is.

While Jesus does not struggle with his identity, you and I sometimes do. We live in unprecedented times. Never before have we fallen to temptation in such a way that we allow emotion to become the determining factor of identity.

Identity can be one of the great challenges in life. Many of us seek to prove who we are through success, status, or some other accomplishment. Many of us cling to who we once were. Many of us cling to external things, such as beauty or size or body image.

We can struggle with our identity through the common challenges of aging. We may struggle to let go of the ways we were once "somebody," and letting go can sometimes feel like we're losing our identity. We may struggle with our identity through a midlife crisis, an empty nest, retirement, or any major transition in life. Many of us define ourselves by our past and fear that we are the sum of our sins and failures.

Here is the good news: None of those things make us who we are. Our identity is received, not earned. Let me explain. I forever will be the son of Prosper J. Toups, Jr. That is an identity that was forged at my conception. No emotion, event, or anything else in life can change that predetermined identity. My identity as the son of a particular father was received, not earned.

Our identity is—and can only be—determined by God. No emotion or interior confusion determines who we are. No success or failure determines or affects how God sees us. No conversion or sin determines or affects how God sees us. There is nothing we can do to impress God. There is nothing we can do to repulse God. Because of the truth of who God is, we can only understand who we are from him.

For Your Prayer

Read Isaiah 62. Read it three times very slowly. What word or phrase tugs at your heart? Talk to God about how this word or phrase applies to your life.

What words stood out to you as you prayed?
What did you find stirring in your heart?

_____

_____

_____

_____

_____

_____

_____

_____

_____

_____

_____

_____

_____

_____

_____

_____

_____

_____

_____

_____

_____

_____

Awe

"When the disciples heard this, they fell
prostrate and were very much afraid."

– MATTHEW 17:6

Monday of the Second Week of Lent

In October 2004, I had the privilege of meeting St. John Paul the Great. During the flight from the United States to Italy, I had hours to consider the reality of what was soon going to happen. I considered all that characterized the life of Pope John Paul II. I recalled his influence on the conversion of Russia and the eventual downfall of the Soviet Union. I considered his landmark teaching on the Theology of the Body. I remembered all the World Youth Days, the reclaiming of orthodoxy on the heels of the Second Vatican Council, the reform of seminaries, and his tireless ministry to priests.

As I was born in 1972 and he was elected Vicar of Christ in 1978, John Paul II was the only pope I really knew. It was with great anticipation and reverence for his vast accomplishments that I prepared for my face-to-face encounter with him.

The moment, while brief, was profound. However, it was distinct for reasons that might be surprising. John Paul II died in April 2005. My meeting with him occurred six months before his death. Instead of encountering a refined statesman who commanded the international stage, I was face to face with a man dying of Parkinson's disease. Here I stood before John Paul II, a man who taught the world how to live and who was now teaching the world how to die.

The moment was wrapped in silence. It was profound. I was in awe. Awe is what you experience when you are in the presence of something so powerfully transcendent that you feel small and speechless.

For the Apostles, the experience of the Transfiguration was so powerful that they fell on their faces, filled with awe. I do not know about you, but I would love to have an experience of God so powerful that I fell on my face because I was filled with awe.

When was the last time that you were in awe of God? When was the last time you were awe of anything or anyone?

Self-absorption kills awe. Self-absorption threatens a vibrant relationship with God. Many of us tend to live in self-absorbed worlds where we are the center of our concern, our conversation, and our social media posts. This narcissistic posture of "me" is, for many of us, the posture that most threatens our relationship with God.

Today, ask God for the grace to stop being absorbed in yourself and your circumstances. Ask him to renew your awe of him and all that he is.

For Your Prayer

Read Isaiah 43:1–7. Read it three times very slowly. What word or phrase tugs at your heart? Talk to God about how this word or phrase applies to your life.

What words stood out to you as you prayed?
What did you find stirring in your heart?

Trust

*"But Jesus came and touched them,
saying, 'Rise, and do not be afraid.'"*

– MATTHEW 17:7

F ear is a natural part of life. In the people we read about in the Bible, fear is one of the more common experiences.

Theophany is a biblical term that describes an event when God reveals himself to man. There are 365 theophanies in the Bible. Interestingly enough, the most common theme of them all is God's opening line: "Do not be afraid." Why? When we are in awe of God, the common emotion is fear. The good news is this: when God senses our fear, his most common response is "Do not be afraid."

God wants us to not be afraid. Far too many of us know the reality of fear. Sometimes that fear is a direct response to his presence, as in a theophany, but often that fear is simply from the ordinary rhythm of life. Many of us know well what it feels like to struggle with anxiety and fear.

It would be easy for us to mistake Jesus' words "Do not be afraid" as mere encouragement or an invitation to positive thinking. But this is not what Jesus is saying. When Jesus says "Do not be afraid," what Jesus is really saying is "Trust me."

The antidote for fear is not courage but trust. Courage, while important in the spiritual life, is about you and what you are doing. Trust, on the other hand, is about a Person—the Person we do not have to fear.

Most often in life our fear is focused on circumstances: "I'm afraid this will happen" or "I'm afraid that will happen." The focus is on the external circumstances. Trust is not focused on circumstances. Trust is focused on the Person who is with me in the midst of the circumstances. Far too often I cannot change my circumstances, nor can I make those circumstances go the way I want them to go.

I can, however, trust a Person. I can trust God who is with me regardless of the circumstances. I can trust God who is who he says he is. I can trust God who is more powerful than whatever I am facing. I can trust that God is fully aware of my circumstances.

For Your Prayer

Read Psalm 121. Read it three times very slowly. What word or phrase tugs at your heart? Talk to God about how this word or phrase applies to your life.

What words stood out to you as you prayed?
What did you find stirring in your heart?

_____

_____

_____

_____

_____

_____

_____

_____

_____

_____

_____

_____

_____

_____

_____

_____

_____

_____

_____

_____

_____

_____

_____

Understand

"As they were coming down from the mountain, Jesus charged them, 'Do not tell the vision to anyone until the Son of Man has been raised from the dead.'"

– MATTHEW 17:9

Today we wrap up our study of the Gospel from the Second Sunday of Lent. At the conclusion of the Transfiguration, Jesus instructs the Apostles, "Do not tell the vision to anyone until the Son of Man has been raised from the dead."

Peter, James, and John heard this, but there is no guarantee that they fully understood it. They did not understand why they should tell no one, nor did they understand what Jesus meant when he said "raised from the dead." The Gospels are filled with the humanity of the Apostles, who followed Jesus unreservedly but often did not fully understand him.

Yesterday, we talked about trust. There is an important connection between understanding and trusting. We do not trust in circumstances; we trust a Person—Jesus. If we are going to trust the person, then it is important for us to not confuse clarity with understanding.

I can be clear that Jesus is asking me to do something, but I may not understand why he is asking me to do it or what the next step is. Let me give you an example. In the summer of 2021, I was able to take a long-awaited and well-deserved six-month sabbatical for further study and spiritual renewal. I cherished the gift of time and the reality of a full six months away. During the fourth month of the sabbatical (in July), I began to sense that the Lord was saying, "I want to be the only security you have." I did not understand this, but I trusted the words because I trusted the Person who spoke the words.

Halfway through the fifth month of the sabbatical (in August), I felt the Lord bringing the sabbatical to a close. This was a great surprise, because I was fully expecting to be away for the full six months. Again, I did not understand it, but I trusted the words because I trusted the One who spoke them. My sabbatical began on April 1 and the fifth month ended on August 31.

On August 29, 2021, Hurricane Ida made landfall in Louisiana as the most powerful hurricane on record in history in Louisiana. The storm passed right over the church where I was pastor. While I had not understood the words the Lord said to me in July and early August, I trusted those words. It was only now that I came to understand why he said those words to me.

Many of us equate understanding with trust, and while understanding might fulfill an inner need to be in control, God does not work like that. God understands, so I do not have to. If I really trust him—and if I really believe that he only wants what is best for me—then once it is clear what he wants me to do, my only response is to say yes. I say yes to God even when I do not fully understand.

For Your Prayer

Read John 21:15–19. Read it three times very slowly. What word or phrase tugs at your heart? Talk to God about how this word or phrase applies to your life.

What words stood out to you as you prayed?
What did you find stirring in your heart?

_____

_____

_____

_____

_____

_____

_____

_____

_____

_____

_____

_____

_____

_____

_____

_____

_____

_____

_____

_____

_____

_____

Take a moment to reflect on the past week, going over the meditations that bore the most fruit in your prayer, the things you wrote, and your reflections from the video.

The Samaritan Woman

FIRST READING

Exodus 17:3–7

In those days, in their thirst for water, the people grumbled against Moses, saying, "Why did you ever make us leave Egypt? Was it just to have us die here of thirst with our children and our livestock?" So Moses cried out to the LORD, "What shall I do with this people? A little more and they will stone me!"

The LORD answered Moses, "Go over there in front of the people, along with some of the elders of Israel, holding in your hand, as you go, the staff with which you struck the river. I will be standing there in front of you on the rock in Horeb. Strike the rock, and the water will flow from it for the people to drink. This Moses did, in the presence of the elders of Israel.

The place was called Massah and Meribah, because the Israelites quarreled there and tested the LORD, saying, "Is the LORD in our midst or not?"

RESPONSORIAL PSALM

Psalm 95:1–2, 6–7, 8–9

R. *If today you hear his voice, harden not your hearts.*

Come, let us sing joyfully to the LORD;
  let us acclaim the Rock of our salvation.
Let us come into his presence with thanksgiving;
  let us joyfully sing psalms to him.

Come, let us bow down in worship;
  let us kneel before the LORD who made us.
For he is our God,
  and we are the people he shepherds, the flock he guides.

Oh, that today you would hear his voice:
  "Harden not your hearts as at Meribah,
as in the day of Massah in the desert,
  where your fathers tempted me;
they tested me though they had seen my works."

SECOND READING

Romans 5:1–2, 5–8

Brothers and sisters: Since we have been justified by faith, we have peace with God through our Lord Jesus Christ, through whom we have gained access by faith to this grace in which we stand, and we boast in hope of the glory of God.

And hope does not disappoint, because the love of God has been poured out into our hearts through the Holy Spirit who has been given to us. For Christ, while we were still helpless, died at the appointed time for the ungodly. Indeed, only with difficulty does one die for a just person, though perhaps for a good person one might even find courage to die. But God proves his love for us in that while we were still sinners Christ died for us.

GOSPEL

John 4:5–42

Jesus came to a town of Samaria called Sychar, near the plot of land that Jacob had given to his son Joseph. Jacob's well was there. Jesus, tired from his journey, sat down there at the well. It was about noon.

A woman of Samaria came to draw water. Jesus said to her, "Give me a drink." His disciples had gone into the town to buy food.

The Samaritan woman said to him, "How can you, a Jew, ask me, a Samaritan woman, for a drink?—For Jews use nothing in common with Samaritans.—Jesus answered and said to her, "If you knew the gift of God and who is saying to you, 'Give me a drink,' you would have asked him and he would have given you living water."

The woman said to him, "Sir, you do not even have a bucket and the cistern is deep; where then can you get this living water? Are you greater than our father Jacob, who gave us this cistern and drank from it himself with his children and his flocks?" Jesus answered and said to her, "Everyone who drinks this water will be thirsty again; but whoever drinks the water I shall give will never thirst; the water I shall give will become in him a spring of water welling up to eternal life."

The woman said to him, "Sir, give me this water, so that I may not be thirsty or have to keep coming here to draw water."

Jesus said to her, "Go call your husband and come back." The woman answered and said to him, "I do not have a husband." Jesus answered her, "You are right in saying, 'I do not have a husband.' For you have had five husbands, and the one you have now is not your husband. What you have said is true."

The woman said to him, "Sir, I can see that you are a prophet. Our ancestors worshiped on this mountain; but you people say that the place to worship is in Jerusalem." Jesus said to her, "Believe me, woman, the hour is coming when you will worship the Father neither on this mountain nor in Jerusalem.

You people worship what you do not understand; we worship what we understand, because salvation is from the Jews. But the hour is coming, and is now here, when true worshipers will worship the Father in Spirit and truth; and indeed the Father seeks such people to worship him. God is Spirit, and those who worship him must worship in Spirit and truth."

The woman said to him, "I know that the Messiah is coming, the one called the Christ; when he comes, he will tell us everything." Jesus said to her, "I am he, the one speaking with you."

At that moment his disciples returned, and were amazed that he was talking with a woman, but still no one said, "What are you looking for?" or "Why are you talking with her?" The woman left her water jar and went into the town and said to the people, "Come see a man who told me everything I have done. Could he possibly be the Christ?" They went out of the town and came to him. Meanwhile, the disciples urged him, "Rabbi, eat." But he said to them, "I have food to eat of which you do not know." So the disciples said to one another, "Could someone have brought him something to eat?"

Jesus said to them, "My food is to do the will of the one who sent me and to finish his work. Do you not say, 'In four months the harvest will be here'? I tell you, look up and see the fields ripe for the harvest. The reaper is already receiving payment and gathering crops for eternal life, so that the sower and reaper can rejoice together. For here the saying is verified that 'One sows and another reaps.' I sent you to reap what you have not worked for; others have done the work, and you are sharing the fruits of their work."

Many of the Samaritans of that town began to believe in him because of the word of the woman who testified, "He told me everything I have done." When the Samaritans came to him, they invited him to stay with them; and he stayed there two days. Many more began to believe in him because of his word, and they said to the woman, "We no longer believe because of your word; for we have heard for ourselves, and we know that this is truly the savior of the world."

Pursue

*"Jesus came to a town of Samaria ... [and]
sat down there at the well."*

– JOHN 4:5–6

Thursday of the
Second Week of Lent

Our attention shifts today as we transition from the Gospel of the Second Sunday of Lent and prepare for the Gospel of the Third Sunday. As we do so, we leave the Gospel of Matthew and enter the Gospel of John. In John 4, we read the famous account of Jesus with the Samaritan woman at the well.

Understanding the geography in the story will help us appreciate the theology of the message. Jesus is walking with his disciples, and he intentionally leads them to Samaria. Jews and Samaritans had nothing to do with each other, so one can imagine that Sychar is the last place the Apostles expect Jesus to take them. But Jesus does nothing without a specific intention. When Jesus arrives in Samaria, he knows full well what he will find when he gets there. He is there for a reason. He is there to pursue sinners.

A few days ago, I shared with you my favorite quote from the *Catechism*: "God calls man first. Man may forget his Creator or hide far from his face; he may run after idols or accuse the deity of having abandoned him; yet the living and true God tirelessly calls each person to that mysterious encounter known as prayer. In prayer, the faithful God's initiative of love always comes first; our own first step is always a response" (CCC 2567).

Why do I cherish this as I do? Why is this teaching so important to me? This particular line describes so much of my life: "Man may forget his Creator or hide far from his face; he may run after idols or accuse the deity of having abandoned him." I know painfully what it is like to forget God. I know well when I hide and how I hide and why I hide from God. I have far too often had to deal with the consequences of running after idols. And when all these things happen, instead of taking responsibility for my own actions, I often project my frustration onto God and accuse him of having abandoned me.

I know all this to be true. But the good news is found in these words: "Yet the living and true God tirelessly calls each person to that mysterious encounter known as prayer."

It is God who takes the initiative in our lives. It is God who pursues us, not we who pursue God. God is in control, not you or me. God is pursuing me and is doing so tirelessly.

The entire experience of Lent is leading us to the Cross, where Jesus will show us the full extent of his pursuit of us. Be not afraid; Jesus is pursuing you.

Stop. Slow down. Be still. Let him find you. He is pursuing you.

For Your Prayer

*Read John 4:5–15. Read it three times very slowly.
What word or phrase tugs at your heart? Talk to God
about how this word or phrase applies to your life.*

What words stood out to you as you prayed?
What did you find stirring in your heart?

Hide

"Jesus ... sat down there at the well. It was about noon. A woman of Samaria came to draw water."

– JOHN 4:6–7

Friday of the Second Week of Lent

Jesus encounters the Samaritan woman at the well as she comes to draw water at noon. This detail is important. People did not go to the well at noon. It was too hot. They would draw water early in the morning, and then again at sunset. But the woman is there at noon precisely because no one else would be there. She is a sinner. She is there at noon because she does not want anyone to see her. She is hiding.

The most common response to sin is to hide. In Genesis 3, after they have sinned, Adam and Eve hide from God. In their shame, they cover their nakedness to hide their bodies from each other. We do the same, don't we?

Let me share with you a particular story. Just two days ago I shared my experience of having to return home from sabbatical a month early because of the unexpected landfall of Hurricane Ida. The first five months of sabbatical were filled with profound grace. The Lord's presence was near. His voice was clear. Unfortunately, Hurricane Ida forced me to leave early. I returned to chaos and destruction. The scenes that awaited me at home couldn't have been more different from the peace of my sabbatical.

To be honest, I was angry that I had to come home early. I was angry to come home to Hurricane Ida. I was angry that the ease and the peace of sabbatical was taken away. And I was shocked by how fast my emotions changed. It was as if one day I was swimming in gratitude for all that God had done, and the next day my heart had forgotten the gratitude and was only angry at the present circumstances. In time, I grew ashamed of my anger at God, and I begin to hide from him. I stopped praying for a bit because I was "too busy." I stopped talking to him, much less desiring to hear him speak back.

When we sin, the shame and inner accusation are often too much for us to bear, so we hide from God. We not only hide from God, but we also attempt to hide our sin though overcompensation or spiritual achievement, hoping that once we get our lives back in order, then God will love us. Sound familiar?

Attempting to hide, the Samaritan woman comes face to face with a God who pursues her in her hiding. You and I are the "woman at the well" in today's Gospel. Be not afraid. God does not pursue us because we are worthy. God pursues us because he loves us, and God loves us most in the places where we feel we need to hide.

For Your Prayer

Read John 4:5–26. Read it three times very slowly.
What word or phrase tugs at your heart? Talk to God
about how this word or phrase applies to your life.

What words stood out to you as you prayed?
What did you find stirring in your heart?

Search

"Jesus answered her, 'You are right in saying, "I do not have a husband." For you have had five husbands, and the one you have now is not your husband.'"

– JOHN 4:17–18

Yesterday, we mentioned that the woman at the well did not want anyone to see her. Today, we discover why.

Jesus tells her that she has had five husbands and that the man she is living with now is not her husband. She has a past, and all indications are that she is running from her past. We cannot know why she has had so many husbands, but we can speculate that because she is hiding from the rest of the community, there is something in her past that is troubling or gripping her with shame.

Let's go a bit deeper. Sin is often medicinal. I take medicine, ibuprofen, when I have a headache. The medicine numbs the pain. Likewise, much sin is medicinal; it seeks to numb a pain within us. The Bible does not tell us why the Samaritan woman struggles with promiscuity. What is clear, though, is that she is searching for something to fill a void within.

She is searching for something or someone. Perhaps she is searching for something or someone to numb the pain. Many of us run from God's pursuit of us and attempt to hide from him because we are ashamed of our past—or at least of something that continues to affect how we see ourselves in the present. Many of us are afraid that when God finds out about our past, he will abandon us. This fear is what leads to the hiding.

God is forever pursuing us, and at some point he will find us. When God finds us, many of us may expect our deepest fear to come to fruition. But what God says when he finds us is "Do not be afraid."

Do not be afraid. Not afraid. All he says to us is "Do not be afraid."

I am willing to bet that most of your mistakes were fueled by something that you were searching for. I am willing to bet that most of your pain in life is rooted in something that you were searching for that you did not find. We are all searching for God.

In Jesus, we come to see that we have been searching for someone, not something.

Today, trust the process and trust the person. With Jesus, look at your history of sin and your most predominant sins. What is underneath the sin? What is the pattern? What have you been searching for?

For Your Prayer

Read John 4:5–42. Read it very slowly. What word or phrase tugs at your heart? Talk to God about how this word or phrase applies to your life.

What words stood out to you as you prayed?
What did you find stirring in your heart?

_____

_____

_____

_____

_____

_____

_____

_____

_____

_____

_____

_____

_____

_____

_____

_____

_____

_____

_____

_____

Thirsty

"The woman said to him, 'Sir, give me this water, so that I may not be thirsty.'"

– JOHN 4:15

In the 1995 film *The American President*, there is a poignant conversation between two main characters, Andrew Shepherd, the president of the United States, and his advisor, Lewis Rothschild. Lewis is attempting to inspire the President to do something that he himself thinks is important. As a trusted advisor, Lewis says to the President, "People want leadership. They're so thirsty for it they'll crawl through the desert toward a mirage, and when they discover there's no water, they'll drink the sand."

President Shepherd responds, "People don't drink the sand because they're thirsty. They drink the sand because they don't know the difference."

We are all searching. I am searching. You are searching. You would not be reading this book if you were not searching for something. We are all thirsty. We are so thirsty, in fact, that we will struggle through the desert toward a mirage, and when we discover there is no water there, we will indeed drink the sand.

Far too many of us crawl through life seeking the mirages, believing whatever promises to quench our thirst. The woman at the well has tried to quench her thirst with men. We all share have in common with her in that we have all tried to quench our thirst with something—control, possessions, or status, among other things. Each of us has our patterns. Maturity is knowing what they are.

Here's the thing about mirages, the thing about temptation. A mirage looks very enticing when you're thirsty in the desert. But even though it looks like something we desire, it is not what it appears to be. It is a mirage. The mirage cannot give us the very thing it promises because the mirage in itself is nothing.

Temptation is the same. Temptation will never follow through on its promise. Temptation promises that it will quench our thirst. Temptation promises us that it will make us happy. But just as the mirage cannot deliver on its promise, temptation cannot deliver on its promise either. That is the nature of temptation. It always overpromises and under-delivers.

What is more sobering is the fact that we know this, and we still pursue it. We know that the mirage is a mirage. We know that there is only sand. But when you're that thirsty in the desert, you see a mirage and you drink the sand.

Again today, trust the process and trust the Person. With Jesus, look at your history of sin and your most predominant sins. What are the mirages that promise to make your life better but only leave you thirsty?

For Your Prayer

Read Psalm 63. Read it very slowly. What word or phrase tugs at your heart? Talk to God about how this word or phrase applies to your life.

What words stood out to you as you prayed?
What did you find stirring in your heart?

Person

"Jesus said to her, 'I am he, the one who is speaking with you.'"

– JOHN 4:26

Monday of the Third Week of Lent

Today we continue to unpack the Gospel from the Third Sunday of Lent. Jesus is at the well with this woman who has been married five times and is now living with a man who is not her husband. She says, "I know that the Messiah is coming, the one called the Christ." And Jesus reveals to her that he is the Messiah. He says, "I am he, the one who is speaking with you." In a sense, Jesus is saying, "I am the one you are searching for. I am the one who can fill the emptiness inside. I am the one who can quench your thirst."

I. Jesus.

Jesus is the only religious leader in human history who intentionally leads people to himself. He is the answer. Christianity is about a Person. On the second day of our journey together, I shared with you the words of Pope Benedict XVI from his encyclical *God Is Love*: "Being Christian is not the result of an ethical choice or a lofty idea, but the encounter with an event, a person, which gives life a new horizon and a decisive direction."[7]

Jesus Christ wants a personal relationship with you—and so much more than that. Imagine what your life would look like if by the end of Lent you had a much more intimate relationship with God then you do today. Imagine what your life would look like if your relationship with God were more personal and more vibrant. Do you want this? And if so, how much do you want it?

He is pursuing you, even in your hiding and searching and thirsting. You were made for a Person, not an idea. The woman at the well was longing for a Person—the Messiah. You and I are longing for a Person—Jesus, who knows everything about you and still pursues you.

Again today, trust the process and trust the Person of Jesus. The reality is this: developing a deeply personal relationship with Jesus requires the same relational dynamics as developing a personal relationship with a human being in your life. Deacon James Keating, PhD, writes, "It is in this divine self-giving and the positive human response to accept such love that healing is known. Trust, vulnerability, rapt listening, integrity all precede the fullness of healing; otherwise God could incorrectly be seen as entering a magic relationship and not one of human freedom and fulness. We must present ourselves in such a way that Christ can enter our heart with truth. And such a way of presenting oneself is encapsulated in the virtue of humility."[8]

What is the one thing you are, or have been, most afraid to share with Jesus? Today—yes, today—have the conversation with Jesus. Be not afraid.

For Your Prayer

Read Psalm 139:1–16. Read it three times very slowly. What word or phrase tugs at your heart? Talk to God about how this word or phrase applies to your life.

What words stood out to you as you prayed?
What did you find stirring in your heart?

_____

_____

_____

_____

_____

_____

_____

_____

_____

_____

_____

_____

_____

_____

_____

_____

_____

_____

_____

_____

_____

_____

Hope

"He told me everything I have done."

– JOHN 4:39

The conversation that unfolds between Jesus and the Samaritan woman at the well is interesting indeed. Jesus reveals the truth of who he is and what that truth means for her. It is Jesus revealing all he knows about her that transforms her life. She is known, and more importantly she is loved in the reality of her broken life.

Let's appreciate her response to being fully known by God. The woman, transformed by this experience, cannot help but share the Good News. She has encountered a person, and this person has changed her life. She now has hope.

What is fascinating is how she expresses her hope. She proclaims, "He told me everything I have done." Her hope is not that God will not find out. Her hope—her joy!—is that she is known and loved particularly in her sins. She is known and loved by God! She is loved not in spite her sins but precisely in her sins.

This is important because what is true about her is true about so many of us. Our deepest fear is that God won't love us if he discovers our sins. We fear that he will abandon us. We fear that we are alone. Still more, what paralyzes us is not what we have done but how what we have done determines who we are.

You may have heard someone say, "They only call it mercy when you don't deserve it." It's true. The Samaritan woman has done nothing to earn the gift Jesus gives her; she does not "deserve" to have her sins forgiven. But Jesus is pure love, pure mercy. And they only call it mercy when you do not deserve it.

We all need mercy. Mercy has a name—Jesus. At the well, Jesus does not erase the woman's past; he simply transforms the moment and frees her from the prison of isolation in which she was living. She knows that she is no longer alone, and she knows that, even as a sinner, she can experience love.

Again today, trust the process and trust the Person.

As you look deep within, ask what the one place in your life is, either in your past or your patterns, where you feel or have felt most alone? Do not be afraid. Have hope. Ask Jesus to enter that place in your heart.

For Your Prayer

Read Romans 8:14–39. Read it three times very slowly. What word or phrase tugs at your heart? Talk to God about how this word or phrase applies to your life.

What words stood out to you as you prayed?
What did you find stirring in your heart?

Mercy

"Many of the Samaritans of that town began to believe in him."

– JOHN 4:39

Pope Paul VI once said, "Modern man listens more willingly to witnesses than to teachers, and if he does listen to teachers, it is because they are witnesses."[9] The Samaritan woman has had her life changed by a person, Jesus Christ, who pursued her, revealed what she was thirsty for, and gave her hope. She cannot *not* spread the Good News. She has encountered love. She has encountered mercy.

I mentioned yesterday that they only call it mercy when you don't deserve it. The Samaritan woman did nothing to earn the mercy she received. She did not deserve to have her sins forgiven. But Jesus is pure love, pure mercy. And they only call it mercy when you do not deserve it.

Pope Francis helps us appreciate this when he writes, "Forgiveness is the most visible sign of the Father's love, which Jesus sought to reveal by his entire life. Every page of the Gospel is marked by this imperative of a love that loves to the point of forgiveness. Even at the last moment of his earthly life, as he was being nailed to the Cross, Jesus spoke words of forgiveness: 'Father, forgive them; for they know not what they do' (Luke 23:34)."[10]

Over the past few days, we have had the courage to look deep within our hearts. We have looked at our patterns, our sins, the pains we are medicating. Sometimes when we look that deep within, we hear "excuses" for why Jesus cannot forgive us: "I can't forget." "I haven't done enough." "I don't deserve mercy."

Those things may be true. Maybe you can't forget, but you do not have to. You can never do enough, and you do not have to. And no, you do not deserve God's mercy.

Pope Francis continues, "Nothing of what a repentant sinner places before God's mercy can be excluded from the embrace of his forgiveness. For this reason, none of us has the right to make forgiveness conditional." In fact, when we make God's love conditional, we deny who God really is and incarcerate ourselves in a self-imposed prison. This does not mean that his mercy does not require a response; it simply means that his mercy is not predicated on our worthiness.

Here is the good news, though: they only call it mercy when you do not deserve it.

For Your Prayer

Read Psalm 103. Read it three times very slowly.
What word or phrase tugs at your heart? Talk to God
about how this word or phrase applies to your life.

What words stood out to you as you prayed?
What did you find stirring in your heart?

_____

_____

_____

_____

_____

_____

_____

_____

_____

_____

_____

_____

_____

_____

_____

_____

_____

_____

_____

_____

_____

Take a moment to reflect on the past week, going over the meditations that bore the most fruit in your prayer, the things you wrote, and your reflections from the video.

The Man
Born Blind

FIRST READING

1 SAMUEL 16:1B, 6–7, 10–13A

The LORD said to Samuel: "Fill your horn with oil, and be on your way. I am sending you to Jesse of Bethlehem, for I have chosen my king from among his sons."

As Jesse and his sons came to the sacrifice, Samuel looked at Eliab and thought, "Surely the Lord's anointed is here before him." But the LORD said to Samuel: "Do not judge from his appearance or from his lofty stature, because I have rejected him. Not as man sees does God see, because man sees the appearance but the LORD looks into the heart."

In the same way Jesse presented seven sons before Samuel, but Samuel said to Jesse, "The LORD has not chosen any one of these." Then Samuel asked Jesse, "Are these all the sons you have?" Jesse replied, "There is still the youngest, who is tending the sheep." Samuel said to Jesse, "Send for him; we will not begin the sacrificial banquet until he arrives here." Jesse sent and had the young man brought to them. He was ruddy, a youth handsome to behold and making a splendid appearance. The LORD said, "There—anoint him, for this is the one!"

Then Samuel, with the horn of oil in hand, anointed David in the presence of his brothers; and from that day on, the spirit of the LORD rushed upon David.

RESPONSORIAL PSALM

Psalm 23:1–3a, 3b–4, 5, 6

R. *The Lord is my shepherd; there is nothing I shall want.*

The LORD is my shepherd; I shall not want.
In verdant pastures he gives me repose;
beside restful waters he leads me;
he refreshes my soul.

He guides me in right paths
for his name's sake.
Even though I walk in the dark valley
I fear no evil; for you are at my side
with your rod and your staff
that give me courage.

You spread the table before me
in the sight of my foes;
you anoint my head with oil;
my cup overflows.

Only goodness and kindness follow me
all the days of my life;
and I shall dwell in the house of the LORD
for years to come.

SECOND READING

EPHESIANS 5:8–14

Brothers and sisters: You were once darkness, but now you are light in the Lord. Live as children of light, for light produces every kind of goodness and righteousness and truth.

Try to learn what is pleasing to the Lord. Take no part in the fruitless works of darkness; rather expose them, for it is shameful even to mention the things done by them in secret; but everything exposed by the light becomes visible, for everything that becomes visible is light. Therefore, it says: "Awake, O sleeper, and arise from the dead, and Christ will give you light."

GOSPEL

John 9:1–41

As Jesus passed by he saw a man blind from birth. His disciples asked him, "Rabbi, who sinned, this man or his parents, that he was born blind?"

Jesus answered, "Neither he nor his parents sinned; it is so that the works of God might be made visible through him. We have to do the works of the one who sent me while it is day. Night is coming when no one can work. While I am in the world, I am the light of the world." When he had said this, he spat on the ground and made clay with the saliva, and smeared the clay on his eyes, and said to him, "Go wash in the Pool of Siloam"—which means Sent. So he went and washed, and came back able to see.

His neighbors and those who had seen him earlier as a beggar said, "Isn't this the one who used to sit and beg?" Some said, "It is," but others said, "No, he just looks like him." He said, "I am." So they said to him, "How were your eyes opened?" He replied, "The man called Jesus made clay and anointed my eyes and told me, 'Go to Siloam and wash.' So I went there and washed and was able to see." And they said to him, "Where is he?" He said, "I don't know."

They brought the one who was once blind to the Pharisees. Now Jesus had made clay and opened his eyes on a sabbath. So then the Pharisees also asked him how he was able to see. He said to them, "He put clay on my eyes, and I washed, and now I can see." So some of the Pharisees said, "This man is not from God, because he does not keep the sabbath." But others said, "How can a sinful man do such signs?" And there was a division among them. So they said to the blind man again, "What do you have to say about him, since he opened your eyes?" He said, "He is a prophet."

Now the Jews did not believe that he had been blind and gained his sight until they summoned the parents of the one who had gained his sight. They asked them, "Is this your son, who you say was born blind? How does he now see?" His parents answered and said, "We know that this is our son and that he was born blind. We do not know how he sees now, nor do we know who opened his eyes. Ask him, he is of age; he can speak for himself." His parents said this because they were afraid of the Jews, for the Jews had already agreed that if anyone acknowledged him as the Christ, he would be expelled from the synagogue. For this reason his parents said, "He is of age; question him."

So a second time they called the man who had been blind and said to him, "Give God the praise! We know that this man is a sinner." He replied, "If he is a sinner, I do not know. One thing I do know is that I was blind and now I see." So they said to him, "What did he do to you? How did he open your eyes?" He answered them, "I told you already and you did not listen. Why do you want to hear it again? Do you want to become his disciples, too?" They ridiculed him and said, "You are that man's disciple; we are disciples of Moses! We know that God spoke to Moses, but we do not know where this one is from."

The man answered and said to them, "This is what is so amazing, that you do not know where he is from, yet he opened my eyes. We know that God does not listen to sinners, but if one is devout and does his will, he listens to him. It is unheard of that anyone ever opened the eyes of a person born blind. If this man were not from God, he would not be able to do anything." They answered and said to him, "You were born totally in sin, and are you trying to teach us?" Then they threw him out.

When Jesus heard that they had thrown him out, he found him and said, "Do you believe in the Son of Man?" He answered and said, "Who is he, sir, that I may believe in him?" Jesus said to him, "You have seen him, the one speaking with you is he." He said, "I do believe, Lord," and he worshiped him.

Then Jesus said, "I came into this world for judgment, so that those who do not see might see, and those who do see might become blind." Some of the Pharisees who were with him heard this and said to him, "Surely we are not also blind, are we?" Jesus said to them, "If you were blind, you would have no sin; but now you are saying, 'We see,' so your sin remains."

Eyes

"As Jesus passed by he saw a man blind from birth."

– JOHN 9:1

As we begin preparing for the Gospel of the Fourth Sunday of Lent, our attention shifts today to Jesus' healing of a man who was born blind. The ninth chapter of John opens with what may seem to be an inconsequential statement: "As he passed by, he saw a man blind from his birth." Take note: Jesus *saw* him.

When Jesus beholds the man, he sees him with his eyes. Pope Benedict XVI writes, "Love of neighbor is shown to be possible ... by Jesus. It consists in the very fact that, in God and with God, I love even the person whom I do not like or even know. This can only take place on the basis of an intimate encounter with God. ... Then I learn to look on this other person not simply with my eyes and my feelings, but from the perspective of Jesus Christ. ... Seeing with the eyes of Christ, I can give to others ... the look of love which they crave."[11]

The Holy Father connects our ability to love with our ability to see. It is only when we are able to see people as Jesus sees them that we are able to love people as Jesus loves them. Let me give you a concrete example.

Let's say that someone made many mistakes in the past. And let's say that this person is gripped by shame when they remember their past. This person may consider themselves to be dirty or damaged because of the shameful events of their past.

Let's say again that, later on in their adult life, this person wants to let go of the painful events of the past. As they are trying to do so, the Lord may ask them to forgive themselves as a way of letting go.

What I have come to know in my own life is that we cannot forgive categories. We cannot forgive categories such as "dirty" or "damaged." We can only forgive people.

Therefore, in this particular example, the person would need to see themselves as Jesus sees them, because Jesus sees them as a person, not as a category. Just as with the man born blind, God sees us through his eyes, not ours. His eyes are filled with love and mercy—and as we will discover over the next few days, his eyes are also filled with desire.

Today, take time set apart in silence. Ask yourself, How do you see yourself, through your eyes or God's?

For Your Prayer

Read John 9:1–12 to get familiar with the Gospel reading. Then read Isaiah 43:1–7 (especially verse 4) Read it three times very slowly. What word or phrase tugs at your heart? Talk to God about how this word or phrase applies to your life.

What words stood out to you as you prayed?
What did you find stirring in your heart?

Distort

"His disciples asked him, 'Rabbi, who sinned, this man or his parents, that he was born blind?'"

– JOHN 9:2

Friday of the Third Week of Lent

In ancient Israel, sickness and physical disability were thought to be a direct consequence of sin. So when Jesus encounters the blind man, they ask him, "Rabbi, who sinned, this man or his parents, that he was born blind?"

Jesus' response is worth noting. He says, "Neither he nor his parents sinned: it is so that the works of God might be made visible through him" (John 9:3). He is guiding the conversation to its proper perspective: that he has the power to forgive sins. But we should not dismiss too quickly the disciples' question.

The events described in John 9 show that physical blindness is not necessarily a consequence of personal or generational sin. But we would do well to remember that sin does have consequences, some of which we don't see—namely, sin distorts the way we see ourselves.

From personal experience, both as a priest who has heard more than fifteen thousand confessions and as a penitent, I have come to learn that most of us see ourselves through the lens of our faults. Too many of us assess our self-worth through "what we have done or what we have failed to do." The lens through which we see ourselves is distorted by sin and the consequences of sin in our lives.

Yesterday, we discussed the importance of allowing ourselves to be seen as God sees us. This is important because many of us see ourselves through the distorted lens of our past. Sometimes the distortion comes from what we have done, from sin or ordinary feelings of life. Sometimes the distortion comes from what we have failed to do or from things that did not happen. Sometimes the distortion is because we internalize ways we have failed to meet our own expectations or the expectations of other people. Sometimes the distortion comes from our experience of how other people see us, especially if they have criticized us. We can be labeled by people, by the circumstances in which we were raised, or by the superficial labels of our secular culture.

Trust the process. How do you see yourself? How have your sin or your failings influenced or distorted the way you see yourself?

Today, take time set apart in silence. Ask yourself, How do you see yourself, through your eyes or God's?

For Your Prayer

Read John 9:1–34 to get familiar with the Gospel reading. Then read Zechariah 3:1–7. Read it three times very slowly. What word or phrase tugs at your heart? Talk to God about how this word or phrase applies to your life.

What words stood out to you as you prayed?
What did you find stirring in your heart?

Settle

"His neighbors and those who had seen him earlier as a beggar said, 'Isn't this the one who used to sit and beg?'"

– JOHN 9:8

From the details presented in John's Gospel, we can glean that the man born blind had resigned himself to a life of begging. We know this from the response of those who knew him: "Isn't this the one who used to sit and beg?"

You can almost feel the despair in his heart. The best he can do in life is beg. Instead of dreaming that his life can be all that God intended for his joy and fulfillment, he is resigned. He has settled for far less than what God made him for.

Perhaps he is resigned because he is tired of asking for help. Perhaps he has stopped dreaming because of the pain of feeling that his prayers were not heard. Perhaps he has settled for begging because he has internalized a perception of himself that is fueled by both his physical and emotional limitations. While we do not know why he has resigned himself, these are some of the reasons why we do this in our lives.

Far too many of us settle in life. Most of us start out with dreams of what life will look like in the future. Then we get busy. We get caught up on the treadmill of "keeping up." Soon we lose hope that our dreams will come true. We settle for what small glimpses of joy we can experience in our hearts.

Temptation promises us happiness, only to leave us dissatisfied with yet more sin. The cycle of sin desensitizes us to grace and joy and further distorts the way we see ourselves and life in general. We settle and say, "This is as good as it gets." This begins a slow fade in our interior life. Our joy fades. Our hope fades. And our belief that anything will ever change fades.

This journey of learning is taking place deep inside our hearts. I appreciate your courage in looking deep within. May I ask you to go yet a bit deeper? Ask yourself, Have you settled? Are you happy? Are you really happy? Do you think your life, as you know it now, is as good as it gets? What if there were more? Would you want more?

For Your Prayer

Read John 9:1–41 to get familiar with the Gospel reading. Then read Isaiah 65:1–2. Read it three times very slowly. Consider what these words are saying to you. Talk to God about your life. Ask yourself, Is there more?

What words stood out to you as you prayed?
What did you find stirring in your heart?

_____

_____

_____

_____

_____

_____

_____

_____

_____

_____

_____

_____

_____

_____

_____

_____

_____

_____

_____

_____

_____

_____

_____

More

"So he went ... and came back able to see."

– JOHN 9:7

A few years back, God showed me two images in prayer. The first was an elegant stack of wrapped gifts filling an entire room. As my imagination saw this large stack of gifts, my heart quickened with excitement and I instinctively felt a deep gratitude. I asked him to describe or explain what this large stack of gifts was. He replied, "This stack of gifts represents all of the things that I have blessed you with and all the things you have received from me."

As my prayer continued, a second image was revealed to me. There was a second stack of wrapped gifts. But this stack had a noticeable difference. These gifts were more elaborate, more ornate, and more valuable. Furthermore, there were infinitely more of them. The first stack of gifts was large, but the second stack was as tall as a skyscraper and as deep as the eye could see. The second stacked dwarfed the first stack.

I asked the Lord with great anticipation what the second stack might be. Then I heard this whisper in my heart: "The first stack is what I have blessed you with; the second is all the graces you squandered because you were not ready to receive them."

Whew. Talk about a piercing come out from the Lord. It was then that I realized that I too had settled in life. It's not that I settled for what was bad. I simply settled for what I thought would make me happy. It was then that I realized that there is more.

There is more. There is more to life than living day to day, thinking "this is as good as it gets." There is more than the fatigue that often weighs on us because of the treadmill we are on. There is more freedom, more peace, more joy. It starts with seeing ourselves through the Lord's eyes rather than our own.

Let us imagine for a moment what it would have been like to be born blind and then to all of a sudden be able to see. For the first time, you would be able to see a reality that has been there the whole time but that you were not able to experience.

Imagine how much more you would be able to experience now because you could see. Now let us imagine what more the man in John 9 was able to experience once he "came back able to see."

What if there is a reality that has been there your entire life but that you could not see? Would you want to see? Do you want more?

For Your Prayer

Read John 15:1–11. Read it three times very slowly. What word or phrase tugs at your heart? Talk to God about how this word or phrase applies to your life.

What words stood out to you as you prayed?
What did you find stirring in your heart?

Better

"If he is a sinner, I do not know. One thing I do know is that I was blind and now I see."

– JOHN 9:25

Monday of the Fourth Week of Lent

I am convinced that most people do not ask God for more because they do not truly believe that what God can offer is better than what they can provide for themselves. So let us begin today with a question: Do you believe that what God can provide for you is better than what you are experiencing now?

The man born blind stands before his doubters and speaks frankly: "If he is a sinner, I do not know. One thing I do know is that I was blind and now I see." You can almost hear his thoughts as he speaks: "Look, I don't know about all of your questions. This I know: I was blind, and now I'm not. Jesus healed me, and my life is better."

The more that God wants to give us is not the same "more" that our materialistic minds often perceive. After all, are material things really what life is about? Would more stuff really make us happy?

To understand the more God wants to give us—and how it is far better than what we have settled for—we need to ask him to show us what he sees when he looks at us.

Trust the process. Carve out some time for prayer today. Ask yourself the following question and talk to God about it: Do you believe that what God can and will provide for you is better than what you are experiencing now?

For Your Prayer

Read Ephesians 3:14–20. Read it three times very slowly. What word or phrase tugs at your heart? Talk to God about how this word or phrase applies to your life.

Then invest time in the following spiritual exercise.

First, ask the Lord to show you the times in your life when you were happiest. It could be when you were young, or it could be where you were just a few years ago or where you are now. What made it such a blessed time in your life? Ask the Lord to show you what in those circumstances brought you such joy. Ask the Lord to show you what your heart looked like at that time that made you so happy.

Second, ask the Lord to show you a particular person or persons in your life who you admire the most. What is it about those persons that you have an affection for? What do you sense they have interiorly that you desire in your own heart? Ask the Lord to show you what virtues they espouse that make them so happy.

What words stood out to you as you prayed?
What did you find stirring in your heart?

_____

_____

_____

_____

_____

_____

_____

_____

_____

_____

_____

_____

_____

_____

_____

_____

_____

_____

_____

_____

_____

_____

_____

_____

Trust

"He spat on the ground and made clay with the saliva, and smeared the clay on his eyes, and said to him, 'Go wash in the Pool of Siloam.'"

– JOHN 9:6–7

Tuesday of the Fourth Week of Lent

We read in John 9:6–7 that Jesus "spat on the ground and made clay with the saliva, and smeared the clay on his eyes, and said to him, 'Go wash in the Pool of Siloam.'"

Put yourself in the blind man's situation. A man you do not know comes close to you. You can hear his voice, but without sight all you have is your sense of hearing. You can't see what he's doing.

For much of your life you have been mocked, ridiculed, and humiliated. On a daily basis, people try to steal the money you have collected by begging. You have become oversensitive to people's movements near you because you do not trust them to have the best in mind for you. Because of this, strangers are not safe for you.

Now a stranger, this Jesus, is in front of you. You cannot see what he's doing; you can only hear what is happening. This man you do not know spits in the dirt and makes a pasty clay. Then he presses this clay onto your eyes with his fingers. Think about that. Let that sink in.

Let yourself feel all the emotions that the man born blind would have felt—everything from a desperate hope that this would work to a conditioned fear that perhaps the man was making fun of him. How much trust would you need to let someone put saliva and dirt on your eyes?

To top it off, this man you do not know tells you to go and wash in the sacred pool. Chances are the blind man as already tried to heal himself by washing in the holy waters, only to walk away unhealed and disappointed. How much trust would you need to follow such odd instructions? How much the man born blind must have trusted Jesus!

And Jesus healed the man's blindness. He proved that he is trustworthy.

To you I say, Jesus can be trusted. The "more" he wants for you is better than what you know now. Trust Jesus. Trust his desire for you.

Do you trust God? Are you ready to ask for more?

For Your Prayer

Read Psalm 37:1–7. Read it three times very slowly.
What word or phrase tugs at your heart? Talk to God
about how this word or phrase applies to your life.

What words stood out to you as you prayed?
What did you find stirring in your heart?

_____

_____

_____

_____

_____

_____

_____

_____

_____

_____

_____

_____

_____

_____

_____

_____

_____

_____

"He answered and said, 'Who is he, sir, that I may believe in him?'"

– JOHN 9:36

The story of the man born blind ends with a deeply personal conversation between Jesus and the man who can now see. Jesus asks, "Do you believe in the Son of Man?" The healed man answers, "Who is he, sir, that I may believe in him?"

Jesus has pursued the man for a second time and elicits the question from him. There is something about the asking that is important for the man. Jesus wants him to ask—that's why he prompts him this way. Jesus wants him to ask.

Likewise, Jesus wants you to ask. To ask God for more can make us feel vulnerable. We may wonder, What if God doesn't come through? What if nothing happens? Those questions are actually more about God than they are about us. This is why we began our journey through John 9 asking to see ourselves—and to see God—through his eyes other than our own.

Think about where we have been so far this Lent. Through his Transfiguration, Jesus proves to us that he is who he says he is. Through the story of the Samaritan woman, he reveals that he knows what we are really searching for and what will really quench our thirst. Through the man born blind, Jesus reveals that he is trustworthy.

So why not ask? Ask for freedom. Ask for peace. Ask for joy. Ask for more.

For Your Prayer

Read Matthew 7:7–12. Read it three times very slowly. What word or phrase tugs at your heart? Talk to God about how this word or phrase applies to your life.

Then invest time in the following spiritual exercise.

First, slowly review all that has happened in your life since the beginning of Lent. The story of this Lent is not just the story of the people you have met in the Gospel. It is just as much about you, the person who is reading the Gospel. Take some time to glance through the previous meditations. Which ones made the biggest impact on you? Which days spoke most to your heart?

Second, ask the Lord to show you what he has been saying to you. Ask him to show you what the themes are. Ask him to show you the particular message that he has been revealing to you this past week.

What words stood out to you as you prayed?
What did you find stirring in your heart?

Take a moment to reflect on the past week, going over the meditations that bore the most fruit in your prayer, the things you wrote, and your reflections from the video.

The Raising
of Lazarus

FIRST READING
EZEKIEL 37:12–14

Thus says the Lord GOD: O my people, I will open your graves and have you rise from them, and bring you back to the land of Israel. Then you shall know that I am the LORD, when I open your graves and have you rise from them, O my people!

I will put my spirit in you that you may live, and I will settle you upon your land; thus you shall know that I am the LORD. I have promised, and I will do it, says the LORD.

RESPONSORIAL PSALM
PSALM 130:1–2, 3–4, 5–6, 7–8

R. With the Lord there is mercy and fullness of redemption.

Out of the depths I cry to you, O LORD;
    LORD, hear my voice!
Let your ears be attentive
    to my voice in supplication.

If you, O LORD, mark iniquities,
    LORD, who can stand?
But with you is forgiveness,
    that you may be revered.

I trust in the LORD;
    my soul trusts in his word.
More than sentinels wait for the dawn,
    let Israel wait for the LORD.

For with the LORD is kindness
    and with him is plenteous redemption;
and he will redeem Israel
    from all their iniquities.

SECOND READING

Romans 8:8–11

Brothers and sisters: Those who are in the flesh cannot please God. But you are not in the flesh; on the contrary, you are in the spirit, if only the Spirit of God dwells in you. Whoever does not have the Spirit of Christ does not belong to him.

But if Christ is in you, although the body is dead because of sin, the spirit is alive because of righteousness.

If the Spirit of the one who raised Jesus from the dead dwells in you, the one who raised Christ from the dead will give life to your mortal bodies also, through his Spirit dwelling in you.

GOSPEL (shorter form)

JOHN 11:3–7, 17, 20–27, 33B–45

The sisters of Lazarus sent word to Jesus saying, "Master, the one you love is ill." When Jesus heard this he said, "This illness is not to end in death, but is for the glory of God, that the Son of God may be glorified through it."

Now Jesus loved Martha and her sister and Lazarus. So when he heard that he was ill, he remained for two days in the place where he was. Then after this he said to his disciples, "Let us go back to Judea."

When Jesus arrived, he found that Lazarus had already been in the tomb for four days. When Martha heard that Jesus was coming, she went to meet him; but Mary sat at home. Martha said to Jesus, "Lord, if you had been here, my brother would not have died. But even now I know that whatever you ask of God, God will give you." Jesus said to her, "Your brother will rise."

Martha said, "I know he will rise, in the resurrection on the last day." Jesus told her, "I am the resurrection and the life; whoever believes in me, even if he dies, will live, and everyone who lives and believes in me will never die. Do you believe this?" She said to him, "Yes, Lord. I have come to believe that you are the Christ, the Son of God, the one who is coming into the world."

He became perturbed and deeply troubled, and said, "Where have you laid him?" They said to him, "Sir, come and see." And Jesus wept. So the Jews said, "See how he loved him." But some of them said, "Could not the one who opened the eyes of the blind man have done something so that this man would not have died?"

So Jesus, perturbed again, came to the tomb. It was a cave, and a stone lay across it. Jesus said, "Take away the stone." Martha, the dead man's sister, said to him, "Lord, by now there will be a stench; he has been dead for four days." Jesus said to her, "Did I not tell you that if you believe you will see the glory of God?" So they took away the stone. And Jesus raised his eyes and said, "Father, I thank you for hearing me. I know that you always hear me; but because of the crowd here I have said this, that they may believe that you sent me."

And when he had said this, he cried out in a loud voice, "Lazarus, come out!" The dead man came out, tied hand and foot with burial bands, and his face was wrapped in a cloth. So Jesus said to them, "Untie him and let him go."

Now many of the Jews who had come to Mary and seen what he had done began to believe in him.

longs

"Jesus wept."

– JOHN 11:35

Today our attention shifts as we transition to preparing for the Gospel of the Fifth Sunday of Lent. We remain in the Gospel of John but move from John 9 to John 11. There we read the account of the raising of Lazarus.

There is much to appreciate in the breadth of John 11, as the story of Lazarus covers forty-four verses. Let us enter the scene today at John 11:35, which in only two words tells us much more than we could say in an entire book: "Jesus wept."

Jesus had a great affection for Lazarus. Jesus and Lazarus were best friends. Bethany was close to Jerusalem, and when Jesus taught in the Temple, he would often have stayed at the home Lazarus shared with his sisters, Martha and Mary. Lazarus' home was a safe place for Jesus. He could relax away from the large crowds. Certainly, the affection that he had for his dear friend was behind the tears that we read of in verse 35.

Jesus' tears are tears of longing, not despair. They are tears of mercy and compassion for Lazarus and his family. We see here an awesome mystery: Jesus, in his humanity, expresses the depth of God's love for his friend. Jesus longs for our freedom.

Jesus longs for us to experience the "more" that we were made for. He longs for us to be free from the things that hold us bound so that we can live in a deeply personal relationship with him.

As we journey through the story of Lazarus, these next several days will be our most personal. Why? Deacon Keating writes, "With ever more accurate darts of love the Holy Spirit opens our consciences before God so that deeper and more effective healing can occur; at times His coming is so pure that it causes us to have pain and recoil at the level of intimacy God wishes His Son to achieve in our being. We recoil at our own needed medicine because it will bring about a change, and sin wishes no change to occur."[12]

Sometimes we recoil from God because we fear that he will abandon us. However, you may be surprised to know that we also recoil from God sometimes because he wants to be close to us. When we come face-to-face with the intensity of God's desire for us, many of us can feel uncomfortable precisely because of how personal God wants to be with us.

It is important today to make time to pray with Isaiah 49. Ask God for the grace to feel the intensity of his desire for you. Ask God for the grace to experience just how much he longs for your freedom.

For Your Prayer

Read John 11:1–27 to get familiar with the Gospel reading. Then read Isaiah 49:1–7 and 15–16. Read it three times very slowly. Pay special attention to verse 16. What word or phrase tugs at your heart? Talk to God about how this word or phrase applies to your life.

What words stood out to you as you prayed?
What did you find stirring in your heart?

Afraid

"So Jesus, perturbed again, came to the tomb. It was a cave, and a stone lay across it."

– JOHN 11:38

Jesus made the journey to Bethany because Lazarus had died. As was the custom, Lazarus was buried, his body placed in a tomb that was sealed with a stone.

May I invite you to begin to see the imagery of John 11 through the lens of your life and your heart? With reverence, let us remember that tombs are where we bury someone. We do so with the intent of never again unearthing what is sealed in the tomb.

Many of us have things buried in our hearts. Mistakes. Sins. Omissions and commissions. We may bury the sins we committed as well as the sins committed against us. Many of us have a tomb within, and when we buried those things, we did so with the intent of never again unearthing what was sealed in this tomb.

Listen to me: There is more to life than this. God longs to give you more. And all he asks is permission to enter into the tomb within our hearts.

Returning to the wisdom of Deacon Keating, we read, "For those who have the courage to approach the founts of healing ... the interior life begins to lighten. ... Something greater than the mantras of self-help gibberish and postmodern syncretism is demanded if spiritual healing is to occur. An encounter must occur. We must be seized with the Presence."[13]

"An encounter must occur." God longs for this encounter. God longs to enter the places of our hearts that perhaps we have buried. The stone that lies across our tomb is fear: many of us are afraid of what is there. We spend an inordinate amount of energy protecting ourselves and projecting an image to the world that we have it all under control.

The fear that guards the tomb within, though, has a great influence over who gets close, how and when we push them away, and how we react when we feel threatened.

Today, I ask you to trust the process. What's buried within? What's in the tomb?

For Your Prayer

Read John 11:1–37 to get familiar with the Gospel reading. Then read Ezekiel 36:22–28. Read it three times very slowly. What word or phrase tugs at your heart? Talk to God about how this word or phrase applies to your life.

What words stood out to you as you prayed?
What did you find stirring in your heart?

Unafraid

"Take away the stone."

– JOHN 11:39

Imagine the scene: Jesus arrives and finds a large crowd gathered in Bethany, all of them mourning the death of Lazarus. As he arrives amid the fervor of tears and grief, his presence pierces the noise and his radiating authority silences the crowd.

With an effortless confidence and the authority that transcends human understanding, Jesus strides toward the tomb. Jesus is calm in the midst of the chaos. Jesus is composed, interiorly quiet, and clearly in communion with the Father.

As Jesus stares at the stone outside the tomb, you can feel the energy swirling around the crowd. They are staring at Jesus as he stares at the tomb. You can almost feel the surprise, the sudden catching of breath and the silence, as the people realize that Jesus is about to confront the tomb.

Breaking the silence, Jesus shakes the earth with four words: "Take away the stone."

You can feel the collective shock of the crowd, and then their quick fear of what the tomb will smell like. The crowd is visibly afraid of what is inside the tomb.

Jesus is not afraid of anything. Jesus is not afraid of tombs. Jesus is not afraid of death. Jesus is unafraid.

Jesus knows who he is, and Jesus is who he says he is. He knows the end of the story because he was there with the Father from the beginning of time. He knows that Lazarus will come back to life. He knows that he too will conquer death, victorious over all things in the Resurrection. The tomb is sealed, and the people are afraid, but Jesus is unafraid.

Jesus is unafraid of your tomb. Whatever is buried within, whatever has you bound in fear, Jesus is unafraid of anything you are afraid of. There is nothing he has not already conquered. There is no sin he has not already redeemed.

Right now, this Lent, at this moment of your life, Jesus is knocking on the door your heart with his eyes locked on the door of your tomb. He stands today, unafraid, and with great longing he says to you, "Take away the stone."

For Your Prayer

Read John 11:1–44 to get familiar with the Gospel reading. Then, read Isaiah 54. Read it three times very slowly.

What word or phrase tugs at your heart? Talk to God about how this word or phrase applies to your life.

Then invest in a little more time of prayer today. Close your eyes and ask the Lord to help you imagine the scene described above. Put yourself in the scene there as Jesus raises Lazarus from the dead. Be in the scene as it is happening.

What words stood out to you as you prayed?
What did you find stirring in your heart?

_____

_____

_____

_____

_____

_____

_____

_____

_____

_____

_____

_____

_____

_____

_____

_____

_____

_____

_____

_____

_____

_____

_____

_____

Stench

"Lord, by now there will be a stench; he has been dead for four days."

– JOHN 11:39

By the time Jesus arrives in Bethany, Lazarus has been dead for four days. Imagine the gasp from the crowd when Jesus commands that they remove the stone. They immediately reply, "Lord, by now there will be a stench."

We know there will be a stench, but let us remember the truth of Jesus as he responds, in effect, that he is not afraid of the stench.

I have heard this word before in my own life personally. A few years ago, I was lucky enough to be able to make my second thirty-day silent retreat. During the retreat, there was a stretch of five days when I prayed with the story of the Prodigal Son.

When you are making a thirty-day silent retreat, you pray five times a day for an hour at a time. Over a five-day period, that equates to twenty-five unique one-hour periods of prayer. During that five-day stretch, I prayed with the Prodigal Son twenty-five times. While this was a rare experience, it was also a profound and actually life-changing experience. Jesus was certainly walking with me closely as he and I did a deep review of my life.

As I came face-to-face with my lifelong experience of sin, the image that emerged was a tomb very similar to what I imagine Lazarus's tomb to have looked like. As I continued to pray with this image of a tomb, I knew well what was buried in it. I knew that there was a stench. Buried in that tomb and decaying from years in the dark were the sins that I was most ashamed of.

As I continued to pray over the stretch of days, I found myself in my imagination standing outside this tomb, and I was very aware of my fear of the stench. When I eventually had the courage to ask God to be with me, Jesus stood by my side and stared at my tomb. It was there that I heard words that literally changed my life: "I am unafraid of stench."

We all have a tomb. We all have a stench. When we bury things in the tomb in our hearts, those things rot behind the locked door of fear. Quietly, perhaps even without our knowing it, we can live tormented by a fear of what would happen if we ever went there and opened the tomb. Years may pass, and more things get added to the tomb. The sins we grasp at to medicate the ache within only add to pile inside. Over time we know there's a stench deep within our fear. We resist going there ourselves, and we resist letting God in because "by now there will be a stench."

Jesus is unafraid of stench. You might say his entire mission is to conquer the stench within us. Today, I ask you to trust the process. What is the stench? What unconfessed sins, if any, are buried within? What fears do you need to let Jesus remove from your heart?

What words stood out to you as you prayed?
What did you find stirring in your heart?

_____

_____

_____

_____

_____

_____

_____

_____

_____

_____

_____

_____

_____

_____

_____

_____

_____

_____

_____

_____

_____

_____

Choose

"So they took away the stone."

– JOHN 11:41

Monday of the Fifth Week of Lent

L et us imagine the scene. Jesus stands confidently in front of Lazarus' tomb. He says, "Take away the stone." As he speaks, Jesus' confidence and death's stench collide.

Let us pause now to consider a hidden detail. Jesus does not roll away the stone himself; rather, he asks others to do it. Jesus knows who he is and what he will do, but his words require an act of trust on the part of others in the crowd.

They have to choose. They have to choose to take away the stone. In submitting to Jesus' request, they have to engage their will, actively participating in what Jesus is doing. They chose when "they took away the stone."

It is the same with us and any tomb we have in our heart. Jesus longs for our freedom, but his mercy requires an act of trust on our behalf. We have to choose. We have to choose to roll away the stone or at least give him permission. Jesus isn't a magician, and he will not force himself on us. We have to engage our will to actively participate in what Jesus is doing.

I would like to return to yesterday's story, as I shared with you the experience of standing before my own tomb with Jesus. When I heard Jesus say the words "I am unafraid of stench," I was deeply consoled on the one hand, but on the other hand I was gripped with fear, because I knew well that Jesus was going to open that tomb.

I don't remember many times in my life when I felt more vulnerable before the Lord than in that moment. I knew that I had to give him permission, that I had to choose to let him open the tomb. And I could not do it. I was too afraid. The only word I could muster in my heart as I looked at Jesus was "Help." I said to him, "I can't do this on my own. I need you to help me. I need you to help me give you permission."

That's all I needed to do. That's all he was ever expecting. I had to choose to let him in, but I needed help to do even that. When we struggle to give him permission, remember that all you have to do is ask for help.

Remember the Transfiguration? Jesus proved to us that he is who he says he is. Remember the story of the Samaritan woman? She was transformed in her shame. Remember the story of the man born blind? Jesus proved that he is trustworthy and healed him. Be not afraid. Jesus just needs a crack in the door. Can you choose today to let him in?

For Your Prayer

Again, read Luke 15, except today stay focused on Luke 15:18–20. Read it slowly. Close your eyes. Imagine the scene. Be in the scene. Make a decision as the Prodigal Son did.

What words stood out to you as you prayed?
What did you find stirring in your heart?

Bound

"The dead man came out, tied hand and foot with burial bands, and his face was wrapped in a cloth."

– JOHN 11:44

"The dead man came out, tied hand and foot with burial bands, and his face was wrapped in a cloth." Lazarus was buried. What kept him in the tomb was death, and deep within the stench were bandages that held him bound. Lazarus was bound in death.

Burial bands were a part of ancient Jewish custom. Burial bands would have been wrapped around Lazarus' body. They held him bound.

Often, deep inside our hearts are things holding us bound in a similar way. They prevent us from moving forward. They prevent us from leaving the tomb.

The question for you today is, Where are you bound?

For many of us, deep within the stench are sins that hold us bound. Perhaps we are bound by sins that have never been confessed. Perhaps we are bound by anger, resentment, or unforgiveness toward another person or ourselves, toward life itself or maybe even God. Perhaps we are bound by pain, shame, fear, or lies. Within the tomb in our hearts are things that hold us bound.

Freedom is a very particular gift. I learned a long time ago that there is a difference between freedom *from* and freedom *to*. For me to be free to receive God's love or to follow him wherever he calls, I have to be free from the things that hold me back. The same is true for you. For you to be free to experience the "more" that God is calling you to and all the "more" that life can hold for you, the first step may be to ask the Lord to free you from the things that hold you back.

For us to be free to experience the more that God has in store for us, many of us need to be free from the things that hold us bound. Freedom *to* hinges on freedom *from*.

As I said, freedom is a very particular gift. The things that hold us back are equally personal. The reason most of us don't experience the depth of freedom we long for us because we aren't as specific as we need to be. With great reverence, I invite you to admit and choose to bring to light the particular things that hold you bound.

Freedom awaits. Be not afraid. Today, with Jesus, choose to admit what holds you bound. Do not be afraid to be very specific in naming the things within you that hold you back.

For Your Prayer

Read Luke 7:36–50. Read it very slowly. Close your eyes. Imagine the scene. Be in the scene. Be there, at Jesus' feet. Pay attention to how mercifully he responds.

What words stood out to you as you prayed?
What did you find stirring in your heart?

Unbound

"Untie him and let him go."

– JOHN 11:44

A sk yourself an important question: Why are you alive? Really, ask yourself, Why did God make you?

God does not need humanity—or any of creation, for that matter. The Trinity—Father, Son, and Holy Spirit— has existed through eternity. God is eternal existence; he needs nothing else. Therefore, the only plausible reason that God created man was because he wanted to.

Why did God send Jesus? God is omnipotent; he can do anything he wills. God sent Jesus for the same reason he created us: he wanted to, out of love. God wants us. God longs for us.

Specifically, God longs for our freedom. God longs for us to be unbound.

When speaking of a particular suffering or problem, people often say, "Give that to God." With respect, I do not know how to do that—and I do not find it helpful. What I do find helpful is to say, "God, I give you permission to come in."

God wants to be with us. He longs to be with us. All we have to do is say, "God, I give you permission." God's response is always the same: "Unbind him and let him go."

As we saw yesterday, freedom is a very particular gift. Can you admit, and choose to bring to light, the specific things that hold you bound? Be not afraid. Today, be with Jesus as you were yesterday, and choose to admit what holds you bound.

For Your Prayer

Read John 11:38–44. Read it very slowly. Close your eyes. Imagine the scene. Be in the scene. You are Lazarus. You are in the tomb. Jesus calls you out to be unbound.

Then invest time in the following spiritual exercise.

First, slowly review all that has happened in the past seven days. As I mentioned last Wednesday, the story of this Lent is not just the story of the people you have met in the Gospel. It is just as much about you, the person who is reading the Gospel.

Take some time to glance through the previous six meditations. Which meditations this week made the biggest impact on you? What were the days that spoke most to your heart?

Second, ask the Lord to show you what he himself has been saying to you. Ask him to show you what the themes are. Ask him to show you the particular message that he has been revealing to you this past week.

What words stood out to you as you prayed?
What did you find stirring in your heart?

Take a moment to reflect on the past week, going over the meditations that bore the most fruit in your prayer, the things you wrote, and your reflections from the video.

HOLY WEEK

Hosanna

GOSPEL (AT THE PROCESSION WITH PALMS)

MATTHEW 21:1–11

When Jesus and the disciples drew near Jerusalem and came to Bethphage on the Mount of Olives, Jesus sent two disciples, saying to them, "Go into the village opposite you, and immediately you will find an ass tethered, and a colt with her. Untie them and bring them here to me. And if anyone should say anything to you, reply, 'The master has need of them.' Then he will send them at once."

This happened so that what had been spoken through the prophet might be fulfilled: *Say to daughter Zion, "Behold, your king comes to you, meek and riding on an ass, and on a colt, the foal of a beast of burden."*

The disciples went and did as Jesus had ordered them. They brought the ass and the colt and laid their cloaks over them, and he sat upon them. The very large crowd spread their cloaks on the road, while others cut branches from the trees and strewed them on the road. The crowds preceding him and those following kept crying out and saying: "Hosanna to the Son of David; blessed is he who comes in the name of the Lord; hosanna in the highest."

And when he entered Jerusalem the whole city was shaken and asked, "Who is this?" And the crowds replied, "This is Jesus the prophet, from Nazareth in Galilee."

FIRST READING

ISAIAH 50:4–7

The Lord GOD has given me
  a well-trained tongue,
that I might know how to speak to the weary
  a word that will rouse them.
Morning after morning
  he opens my ear that I may hear;
and I have not rebelled,
  have not turned back.

I gave my back to those who beat me,
  my cheeks to those who plucked my beard;
my face I did not shield
  from buffets and spitting.

The Lord GOD is my help,
  therefore I am not disgraced;
I have set my face like flint,
  knowing that I shall not be put to shame.

RESPONSORIAL PSALM

PSALM 22:8–9, 17–18, 19–20, 23–24

R. My God, my God, why have you abandoned me?

All who see me scoff at me;
    they mock me with parted lips, they wag their heads:
"He relied on the LORD; let him deliver him,
    let him rescue him, if he loves him."

Indeed, many dogs surround me,
    a pack of evildoers closes in upon me;
they have pierced my hands and my feet;
    I can count all my bones.

They divide my garments among them,
    and for my vesture they cast lots.
But you, O LORD, be not far from me;
    O my help, hasten to aid me.

I will proclaim your name to my brethren;
    in the midst of the assembly I will praise you:
"You who fear the LORD, praise him;
    all you descendants of Jacob, give glory to him;
    revere him, all you descendants of Israel!"

SECOND READING

Philippians 2:6–11

Christ Jesus, though he was in the form of God, did not regard equality with God something to be grasped. Rather, he emptied himself, taking the form of a slave, coming in human likeness; and found human in appearance, he humbled himself, becoming obedient to the point of death, even death on a cross. Because of this, God greatly exalted him and bestowed on him the name which is above every name, that at the name of Jesus every knee should bend, of those in heaven and on earth and under the earth, and every tongue confess that Jesus Christ is Lord, to the glory of God the Father.

GOSPEL (shorter form)

Matthew 27:11–54

Jesus stood before the governor, Pontius Pilate, who questioned him, "Are you the king of the Jews?" Jesus said, "You say so." And when he was accused by the chief priests and elders, he made no answer. Then Pilate said to him, "Do you not hear how many things they are testifying against you?" But he did not answer him one word, so that the governor was greatly amazed.

Now on the occasion of the feast the governor was accustomed to release to the crowd one prisoner whom they wished. And at that time they had a notorious prisoner called Barabbas. So when they had assembled, Pilate said to them, "Which one do you want me to release to you, Barabbas, or Jesus called Christ?" For he knew that it was out of envy that they had handed him over.

While he was still seated on the bench, his wife sent him a message, "Have nothing to do with that righteous man. I suffered much in a dream today because of him."

The chief priests and the elders persuaded the crowds to ask for Barabbas but to destroy Jesus. The governor said to them in reply, "Which of the two do you want me to release to you?" They answered, "Barabbas!" Pilate said to them, "Then what shall I do with Jesus called Christ?" They all said, "Let him be crucified!" But he said, "Why? What evil has he done?" They only shouted the louder, "Let him be crucified!"

When Pilate saw that he was not succeeding at all, but that a riot was breaking out instead, he took water and washed his hands in the sight of the crowd, saying, "I am innocent of this man's blood. Look to it yourselves." And the whole people said in reply, "His blood be upon us and upon our children." Then he released Barabbas to them, but after he had Jesus scourged, he handed him over to be crucified.

Then the soldiers of the governor took Jesus inside the praetorium and gathered the whole cohort around him. They stripped off his clothes and threw a scarlet military cloak about him. Weaving a crown out of thorns, they placed it on his head, and a reed in his right hand. And kneeling before him, they mocked him, saying, "Hail, King of the Jews!" They spat upon him and took the reed and kept striking him on the head. And when they had mocked him, they stripped him of the cloak, dressed him in his own clothes, and led him off to crucify him.

As they were going out, they met a Cyrenian named Simon; this man they pressed into service to carry his cross.

And when they came to a place called Golgotha—which means Place of the Skull—they gave Jesus wine to drink mixed with gall. But when he had tasted it, he refused to drink.

After they had crucified him, they divided his garments by casting lots; then they sat down and kept watch over him there. And they placed over his head the written charge against him: This is Jesus, the King of the Jews. Two revolutionaries were crucified with him, one on his right and the other on his left.

Those passing by reviled him, shaking their heads and saying, "You who would destroy the temple and rebuild it in three days, save yourself, if you are the Son of God, and come down from the cross!" Likewise the chief priests with the scribes and elders mocked him and said, "He saved others; he cannot save himself. So he is the king of Israel! Let him come down from the cross now, and we will believe in him. He trusted in God; let him deliver him now if he wants him. For he said, 'I am the Son of God.'" The revolutionaries who were crucified with him also kept abusing him in the same way.

From noon onward, darkness came over the whole land until three in the afternoon. And about three o'clock Jesus cried out in a loud voice, *"Eli, Eli, lema sabachthani?"* which means, "My God, my God, why have you forsaken me?" Some of the bystanders who heard it said, "This one is calling for Elijah." Immediately one of them ran to get a sponge; he soaked it in wine, and putting it on a reed, gave it to him to drink. But the rest said, "Wait, let us see if Elijah comes to save him." But Jesus cried out again in a loud voice, and gave up his spirit.

And behold, the veil of the sanctuary was torn in two from top to bottom. The earth quaked, rocks were split, tombs were opened, and the bodies of many saints who had fallen asleep were raised. And coming forth from their tombs after his resurrection, they entered the holy city and appeared to many.

The centurion and the men with him who were keeping watch over Jesus feared greatly when they saw the earthquake and all that was happening, and they said, "Truly, this was the Son of God!"

Decision

*"See, I have today set before you life
and good, death and evil."*

– DEUTERONOMY 30:15, NAB

Today marks our thirty-seventh day together. I hope that the previous thirty-six days illustrate my love for your soul and my commitment to help you live in freedom. Today, I ask for your permission to stray from our usual flow and share my heart with you in humility and gratitude.

I have been a priest of Jesus Christ for over twenty years. I wake up every morning and beg for God's help, and I go to bed every night and beg for God's mercy. To be honest, I do not know what your opinion of the priesthood is. Certainly, recent scandals involving priests have done little to build confidence in the reality that the priesthood is not a human institution. But the Church teaches us that every priest, on the day of his ordination, is sacramentally changed. The reality of what happens to a man at his ordination to the priesthood is infinitely beyond what we can fully understand. The newly ordained priest literally stands "in the person of Christ the head" *(in persona Christi capitis)* and acts with Jesus' authority on earth.

In last Sunday's reflection I mentioned that I recently made my second thirty-day silent retreat. There, within the thirty days of complete silence, I grappled with the recent scandals that have plagued the Church. I asked God, "Why did you entrust something as sacred as the Church to the hands of weak human beings?" His response shocked me. He said, "I didn't. I entrusted the Church to the priesthood, which is supposed to be Jesus. I entrusted the Church to men acting *in persona Christi capitis.* There are scandals because priests have forgotten who they are."

God never intends scandal. God intended for you, and the entire Church, to rest in the security of Jesus in his priesthood. With that as a prelude, let me apologize for the recent scandals involving priests. The sins that have scandalized the laity are egregious and intolerable. I ask for your forgiveness on behalf of the entire priesthood for the sins of any priest. I beg you, as one who has walked with you for thirty-six days, to forgive any priest who has ever sinned.

Having made this apology from my heart, I now invite you to trust the Lord Jesus and his priesthood from the deepest recesses of *your* heart. Today, I am asking you to go to Confession before Easter—and receive absolution from the hands of a priest. Over the next few days, I will coach you on what to do. Those of you who regularly celebrate the Sacrament of Reconciliation will appreciate this gift of renewal. For those of us who do not regularly go to Confession, let me meet you where you are and see if we can take a few steps together. Today, we'll take one step.

Some of you may have questions about Jesus, the Bible, and where in the Bible Jesus tells us to go to Confession.* Some of you may struggle with Confession because you do not know what to do or have forgotten what to do. Finally, some of you may struggle because it brings up a lot of emotions, and you do not know what to say.

All of this is okay. Do you remember our very first meditation on Ash Wednesday? God just wants your heart. Relax, we will get you ready.

Be not afraid. I am in this with you. Today, just decide to prepare for freedom by preparing for the Sacrament of Reconciliation. Can you engage your will? Can you decide to say yes to freedom?

*If you struggle with these questions, there are many excellent resources available, including the book *Go in Peace: Your Guide to the Purpose and Power of Confession*, by Mitch Pacwa and Sean Brown (Ascension, 2007).

For Your Prayer

Read Deuteronomy 30:15–20. Read it three times very slowly. What word or phrase tugs at your heart? Talk to God about how this word or phrase applies to your life.

What words stood out to you as you prayed?
What did you find stirring in your heart?

Resistance

*"Has anyone trusted in the Lord
and been disappointed?"*

– SIRACH 2:10, NAB

Friday of the Fifth Week of Lent

When I was a kid, I fell off my bike. The fall injured my ankle, causing a cut that needed more than thirty stitches. While the emergency room nurse prepared my ankle for stitching, she had to apply two shots. The first surprised me with discomfort and pain. So what do you think I did when she tried to give me the second shot? I flinched. The body naturally resists what it fears will be painful. Though I knew it was going to help, I resisted it.

The same is true of our hearts. It is completely understandable to me how one would resist God. I see this all the time as a spiritual director. It happens to all of us, including me. We often resist when God is getting too close to the places deep inside our hearts. But here is the good news: If you pay attention to your resistance, you will discover where God is. We resist because God is getting close. When you are afraid, just remember that God is right there.

As you prepare for the Sacrament of Reconciliation, it is okay to feel lots of things, such as fear, doubt, and anxiety. These are to be expected. Be not afraid. The important thing is not what you feel but where you go with the fear. Talk to God about anything and everything that is in your heart as you prepare for Confession. Be not afraid. God already knows. He can handle anything you share with him, including your resistance.

For Your Prayer

Read Deuteronomy 30:15–20. Read it three times very slowly. What word or phrase tugs at your heart? Talk to God about how this word or phrase applies to your life.

Then invest time in the following spiritual exercise.

First, return to your reflections on all that has happened in your life since the beginning of Lent. If you need to, take some time to glance through the previous meditations and your journaling. Again, ask Jesus to show you what the themes are. Ask him to show you the particular message that he has been revealing to you this Lent.

Second, think deeply about what you have reflected on. What are the themes? What has God been saying to you? Now ask yourself if there are any patterns of fear, resistance, or sin connected to what you have learned about yourself so far this Lent. Often what happens when we pick up a theme in our prayer is that the Lord is revealing a pattern of sin. It could be connected to the theme, or it could be the exact opposite of what the theme is saying. Simply review what you have heard from God, and ask him to reveal any sins that need to be confessed.

What words stood out to you as you prayed?
What did you find stirring in your heart?

Specific

"Against you, you alone, have I sinned."

– PSALM 51:4, NAB

Jesus healed specific people of specific illnesses. Likewise, Jesus forgave specific people of specific sins in specific situations. The things that hold us bound are specific, because those things have a very particular influence over us.

When we choose to live in freedom, we do so within our specific life story. The love of God transcends time and space and is poured forth for all of humanity—but God's love is also specific. God loves you, and the ways you experience his love are unique and particular to you. Likewise, the mercy of God transcends time and space and is poured forth for all of humanity—but his mercy is also specific. God forgives you, and the ways you experience his mercy are unique and particular to you.

Sin is not general or abstract. We sin in specific ways. Likewise, pain is not general or abstract. We are wounded in specific ways. The more specific we are in our confession, the more receptive we are to God's mercy. Choosing to name a sin with clarity, precision, and specificity disposes us to receive the fullness of what God has in store for us. Trust the process and the Person. Let's begin to look deep within and prepare with specificity.

For Your Prayer

Read Psalm 51:1–19. Read it three times very slowly. What word or phrase tugs at your heart? Talk to God about how this word or phrase applies to your life.

Then invest time in the following spiritual exercise.

First, return to your prayer from yesterday. What emerged? Have there been particular sins that you became aware of as part of your journey with the Lord this Lent? If so, what are they? What are they specifically?

Second, ask the Lord to show you any sins you have been afraid to actually name specifically in the Sacrament of Reconciliation. As you review your history of going to Confession, has there ever been a time when you have consciously chosen not to name something because you were afraid or ashamed? If so, have a conversation with God about this. Ask him to reveal to you what exactly you were afraid of. In other words, he already knows. In other words, there's nothing to be afraid of. If you have consciously withheld something, ask him to show you the specific fear.

What words stood out to you as you prayed?
What did you find stirring in your heart?

Introduction to
HOLY WEEK

Welcome to Holy Week. Holy Week is unlike any other week. The next eight days are consecrated and set apart for God.

You'll notice that Mass on Palm Sunday is different from other Masses. The difference helps us to *feel* the difference of Holy Week.

On Palm Sunday, we have an extra Gospel reading. It occurs during the Procession with Palms, just before Mass begins. This reading captures both the beauty and the strangeness of Jesus' entry into the holy city. We read, "The crowds preceding him and those following kept crying out and saying: 'Hosanna to the Son of David; blessed is he who comes in the name of the Lord; hosanna in the highest.' And when he entered Jerusalem the whole city was shaken and asked, 'Who is this?'" (Matthew 21:9–10).

We can imagine singing "Hosanna" with the others. But we also know what they didn't know then. We know that by the end of the week, this man will give his life for us on the Cross. So we, too, are shaken and ask, Who is this?

Who is Jesus to you?

Rescue

"Jesus cried out again in a loud voice, and gave up his spirit."

– MATTHEW 27:50

Palm Sunday

There are many ways to describe what Jesus did for us in his Passion. One way is, he rescued us. You cannot rescue yourself; you are helpless. To be rescued means you are trapped in a very particular situation. We are rescued by specific people at specific times in specific ways. Today, as we read the Passion narrative at Mass, we celebrate the fact that Jesus rescued us.

There are consequences to sin. The Fall of Adam and Eve in Genesis 3 destroyed the perfect union between God and man. Death, which did not exist before Original Sin, signals our separation from God. Humanity cannot restore what was destroyed. No matter how hard we try, we cannot restore what was broken.

Let me share an analogy. I love to fish. Once I catch a fish with the intent to keep it, there is only one inevitable outcome: It is going into my ice chest, and it is not getting out on its own. I have never in my life seen a fish save itself from the ice chest. The only way a fish is getting out of that ice chest is if someone comes to rescue it.

Prior to Jesus' suffering, death, and Resurrection, you and I and all of humanity were enslaved to sin and, well, that's it. We were forever trapped in an ice chest. We were trapped forever ... until someone—Jesus Christ—came to rescue us, to save us.

For Your Prayer

Read the Passion narrative in Matthew 26:14–27:66. Read it once slowly, very slowly. Simply pay attention to your heart as you pray. Talk to God about what's in your heart.

Then invest time in the following spiritual exercise.

Close your eyes and imagine that you are at the Cross. As you begin, ask the Holy Spirit to guide your spiritual senses and help you see what the people there saw and hear what they heard. Ask the Holy Spirit to do the inspiring so that there's less pressure on you to make things happen.

Imagine that you are at the foot of the Cross. You can feel the rugged wood under your hands as you touch it. A trickle of blood drips down the wood of the Cross and gently touches your skin.

As you look up, you take in the reality of Jesus' body on the rugged wood just a few feet above you. Your eyes meet Jesus' eyes. You are look deeply into his eyes as he looks deep into you.

What is in your heart as you look at Jesus on the Cross? Ask him to show you the consequences for all humanity if he had chosen not to do what he did.

What words stood out to you as you prayed?
What did you find stirring in your heart?

_____

_____

_____

_____

_____

_____

_____

_____

_____

_____

_____

_____

_____

_____

_____

_____

_____

_____

_____

_____

_____

_____

Thorough

"I will praise you with all my heart,
glorify your name forever."

– PSALM 86:12, <small>NAB</small>

Monday of Holy Week

As I mentioned last week, I've completed a thirty-day silent retreat following the *Spiritual Exercises* of St. Ignatius of Loyola twice. In addition, as a spiritual director to priests, I've had the privilege of facilitating this retreat for others more than twenty-five times. One of my favorite experiences during the retreat is what is known as a "general confession." Let me explain.

The themes of my most recent retreat were pride, self-sufficiency, and control. It focused on my life since ordination. At the conclusion of the retreat, I made a general confession, in which I confessed all my sins, all the facets of pride, self-sufficiency, and control during my priesthood. While I had previously confessed those sins individually and had received absolution, I now had a deeper understanding of them. The general confession allowed me to receive the objective grace that came to me in the Sacrament of Reconciliation.

As you prepare for the Sacrament of Reconciliation, I recommend that you consider examining your heart closely in preparation for a thorough confession. Some of you may consider a general confession, in which you confess all the sins that have come from any of the things that once held you bound. During this Lent, if you have learned more about the memories, patterns, and ways of thinking that have held you bound, confessing these things and the sins that accompany them can be a great spiritual exercise to dispose you to freedom more completely.

For Your Prayer

*Read Psalm 86. Read it three times very slowly.
Prepare for the Sacrament of Reconciliation.*

If you feel so called, prepare for a general confession.

Then invest time in the following spiritual exercise.

*Return to the guided meditation of yesterday's "For your
prayer" section. Return to the Cross. Once again ask
the Holy Spirit to help you see what the people there
saw, hear what they heard, and feel what they felt.*

*Without trying to repeat the experience of yesterday,
simply return to the guided meditation from
yesterday and follow the instructions again today.*

*At the conclusion of the meditation, as you
are looking Jesus in the eyes, ask him if he
is calling you to a general confession.*

What words stood out to you as you prayed?
What did you find stirring in your heart?

Prepare

"Give thanks to the Lord, for he is good, his mercy endures forever."

– PSALM 118:1, NAB

Tuesday of
Holy Week

My final encouragement to you in preparation for the Sacrament of Reconciliation is to be intentional about finalizing preparation. Practically speaking, this might mean doing a little research on how, when, and where you are going to celebrate Reconciliation. Feel free to call your parish for more information and, if necessary, make a special appointment with your parish priest.

The more important preparation is regarding what you bring to the Lord in the sacrament itself. Today, I would like to offer some very practical things you can do to prepare well.

First, bring a list. Many people, including me, get nervous in the moment. Having a list can alleviate fear, keep you focused, and remind you of things you might otherwise forget.

Second, organize your list, perhaps using the Ten Commandments or the seven deadly sins as a guide. You might organize your list by theme, especially if you gained insight into personal themes in your life this Lent.

Third, start with the big ones. It is human nature to want to hide or bury the sins we are most ashamed of. Instead, start with those. Get them over with so that you can relax. Remember, Jesus is not afraid of your sins.

If you invest in preparing well, you will enjoy the Sacrament of Reconciliation and will help the priest in his ministry of mercy and love. Be not afraid. Freedom awaits!

For Your Prayer

Prepare for the Sacrament of Reconciliation.

Then invest time in the following spiritual exercise.

Return to the guided meditation of "For your prayer" for the last two days. Return to the Cross. Once again, ask the Holy Spirit to help you see what the people there saw, hear what they heard, and feel what they felt.

Without trying to repeat the experience of yesterday and the day before, simply return to the guided meditation and follow the instructions again today.

At the conclusion of the meditation, as you are looking Jesus in the eyes, ask him to speak to you about going to Confession.

What words stood out to you as you prayed?
What did you find stirring in your heart?

_____

_____

_____

_____

_____

_____

_____

_____

_____

_____

_____

_____

_____

_____

_____

_____

_____

_____

_____

_____

_____

"And you yourself a sword will pierce."

– LUKE 2:35, NAB

Wednesday of Holy Week

As we begin today, ask the Holy Spirit to guide your spiritual senses and help you see what the people in the scene saw and hear what they heard. Ask the Holy Spirit to do the inspiring so that there's less pressure on you to make things happen.

Imagine the scene: Jesus is just outside Jerusalem in Bethany. It is Wednesday, the day before Holy Thursday. Jesus knows full well that when he leaves this house on Thursday morning, he will not be coming back. He knows full well that Thursday night's Passover meal—the Last Supper—will be followed, in the garden of Gethsemane, by his agony, betrayal, and arrest. And he knows what will happen then.

Let us imagine that it is Wednesday in Bethany ... and Jesus knows what is coming.

Let us enter the scene on that Wednesday in Bethany. The sun is setting, and Jesus wants to prepare his mother, Mary, for what will happen. In the courtyard outside the house where Mary, Martha, and Lazarus live, Jesus looks at the Blessed Mother and says one word, "Mom." From the tone of his voice, she knows.

Imagine the scene: Jesus, with Mary's hand gently resting on his arm, slowly walks with her in the courtyard. As sunset paints the sky burnt orange and majestic yellow, Jesus speaks to his mother about what is to come.

As they pause, Jesus turns and looks at her. Their eyes will meet again on the Via Dolorosa when he is pinned in pain, when he has fallen yet again under the weight of the Cross. Jesus has this moment now to prepare his mother for what is going to happen.

Mary looks deeply into the eyes of her son. He is stricken with grief. She too is on the verge of tears, partly in grief for the suffering he will endure, partly in gratitude for the fulfillment of the Father's promise to save all of humanity.

Jesus takes her hands in his. As he finishes speaking, Mary whispers to her son, "But you will rise on the third day just as you have told us." Jesus smiles, places his mother's hands on his heart, and looks at her tenderly.

Imagine the scene. Jesus is just outside Jerusalem in Bethany. It is Wednesday, the day before Holy Thursday. Jesus is in the courtyard, alone with Mary. He looks at her and says, "Mom."

For Your Prayer

Today, carve out time alone. Ask the Holy Spirit for help. Close your eyes and imagine that you are there with Jesus as he prepares his mother for what is to come.

What words stood out to you as you prayed?
What did you find stirring in your heart?

_____

_____

_____

_____

_____

_____

_____

_____

_____

_____

_____

_____

_____

_____

_____

_____

_____

_____

_____

_____

_____

Take a moment to reflect on the past week, going over the
meditations that bore the most fruit in your prayer, the things
you wrote, and your reflections from the video.

THE TRIDUUM

Made for More

All

"This is my body that is for you."

– 1 CORINTHIANS 11:24, NAB

Holy Thursday

The previous forty-three days have prepared us for the next four—Holy Thursday through Easter Sunday. Up to this point, you have been invited to consider that you were made for more: more freedom, more peace, more joy, a more abundant life.

In a sense, the spiritual exercises of the past forty-three days have disposed you to receive what Jesus is offering you. You have offered him your heart, the things that held you bound, and the fear that prevented you from a deeper relationship. We have focused on what you are offering him. We will now take a turn as we enter the most sacred days of the liturgical year. Now we will unpack what he is offering you.

At the Last Supper, Jesus instituted the Holy Eucharist, giving us the gift of his Real Presence in Holy Communion. At every Mass, the bread and wine become Christ's Body and Blood. Jesus longs for us so much so that he wants to be fully present to us in Holy Communion.

God wants to live in communion with you. He is offering you everything—all of himself. He holds nothing back. Jesus is offering you all of himself—all his love, all his mercy, all his communion. Tonight, he is offering you all of himself. Are you ready to receive him?

For Your Prayer

Clear your calendar for tonight. Attend tonight's Mass of the Lord's Supper. Make plans to stay after Mass for Eucharistic Adoration. After Mass, during Adoration, thank for the Lord for all that he has done for you this Lent.

In preparation for tonight's experience, let me offer a few words that may assist you. First, call your parish and find out what time Mass is tonight.

Second, there is a lot that will be different about tonight's Mass. There is a special Responsorial Psalm that we will sing at Mass tonight—Psalm 116. As you prepare for Mass, see if you can do a little research and find out more about the Hallel psalms, the psalms Jesus prayed before and during his Passion.

Third, the priest will wash feet at Mass tonight. Again, find out more about why we wash feet, why the foot-washing is significant, and how this is a pre-enactment of the Passion.

Fourth, tonight's Mass will end very differently from what you are used to. Your final bit of research is to find out why the Mass of the Lord's Supper ends the way it does.

Finally, bring this book with you to Eucharistic Adoration tonight. Tonight will be a perfect opportunity for you to look back on all that God has done in your life this Lent.

What words stood out to you as you prayed?
What did you find stirring in your heart?

_____

_____

_____

_____

_____

_____

_____

_____

_____

_____

_____

_____

_____

_____

_____

_____

_____

_____

_____

_____

_____

_____

Consummated

"My Father, if it is possible, let this cup pass from me."

– MATTHEW 26:3, NAB

Good Friday

The ritual of the seder, the Passover meal, is very detailed. One detail is the placement of four cups of wine that must be consumed at key moments of the meal. The first cup is consumed at the conclusion of the first movement of the meal. The second cup is consumed after the story of the Exodus has been told and the food is blessed. The third cup, the "cup of blessing," is consumed after the meal has been eaten, following a petition for the Lord's blessing. The fourth cup, the "cup of consummation," is the sign that the Passover has been fulfilled.

At the Last Supper, Jesus takes a cup and gives it to the disciples, instituting the first Eucharist: "This is my blood of the covenant" (Matthew 26:28). It is the third cup, the cup of blessing. Then we read that "after singing a hymn, they went to the Mount of Olives" (Matthew 26:30). They leave. So when is Jesus going to drink of the cup of consummation?

In the garden of Gethsemane, Jesus prays, "My Father, if it is possible, let this cup pass from me" (Matthew 26:39). Jesus knows well that the New Covenant will be fulfilled—consummated—on the Cross. Thus, in the garden, Jesus asks that this cup "pass from" him. He is referring to the Passover cup of consummation, the moment when his rescue of us will be consummated.

Thus, on the Cross, "in order that the scripture might be fulfilled, Jesus said, 'I thirst.' Now there was a vessel filled with common wine. So they put a sponge soaked in wine on a sprig of hyssop and put it up to his mouth. When Jesus had taken the wine, he said, 'It is finished'" (John 19:28–30). In Latin, "it is finished" is *consummatum est.*

On the Cross, Jesus gives himself as a gift. He gives everything. He gives his life. All for love. All for you and me. Just as the Passover initiated the Old Covenant, Jesus' consummation on the Cross initiates a New Covenant—a communion between God and man.

Today is Good Friday. It is very good, for this is the day where we are loved far beyond what we deserve. We do not deserve it. You do not deserve it. I do not deserve it. But Jesus did it anyway. Because he loves us—and now our communion is consummated forever.

For Your Prayer

Read the Passion John 18:1–19:42. Read it once slowly, very slowly. Simply pay attention to your heart as you pray. Talk to God about what is in your heart.

Return to the guided meditation that was presented in the "For your prayer" section of Palm Sunday's reflection. Return to the Cross. Once again ask the Holy Spirit to help you see what the people there saw, hear what they heard, and feel what they felt.

Without trying to repeat the experience of Palm Sunday, simply return to the guided meditation and follow the instructions again today.

At the conclusion of the meditation, as you are looking Jesus in the eyes, ask him to speak to your heart.

What words stood out to you as you prayed?
What did you find stirring in your heart?

Wait

*"They rested on the sabbath according
to the commandment."*

– LUKE 23:56, NAB

Holy Saturday

Forty-six days ago, we began a journey. Today, on this Holy Saturday, we wait ... for Jesus has died. Today we wait. We heard his voice, experienced his Passion, and encountered his love. We have had quite a journey.

With mystical darkness still blanketing creation (see Mark 15:33), we wait. The darkness of Good Friday still lingers, for this Holy Saturday is filled with waiting. After they laid him in the tomb, "they rested on the sabbath according to the commandment" (Luke 23:56).

The disciples wait. Their wait is filled with questions that compete for attention in the silence. "He said he would rise after three days." "Will he?" "Will he rise?" "What if he doesn't?" "If he does, what does that mean?" "Now that he's dead, what are we supposed to do?"

What about you? In the wait, what do you hear? In the silence, if you can give yourself permission to wait, what rises in your heart? Perhaps you hear questions like "Now what?" "What happens after today?" "What will I do Monday?" "Who will lead me?" The ordinary emotions you're feeling right now are similar to the feelings that the disciples felt as they waited.

Trust the process, for it will help you appreciate the Good News of Easter Sunday. Today, wait in darkness. Feel what it is like to be without him.

For Your Prayer

Rise very early—before sunrise—and wait in the darkness. Sit there, in the darkness, and wait. Meditate on your experiences through this Lenten journey. What were the highlights? What has the Lord done for you?

Then invest time in the following spiritual exercise.

Write a letter to God. As you write, be very specific. What do you want to say to him about your experience of him and your experience of this Lent. Remembering that the blessings have been very specific, make your letter as specific as you can. Ask the Holy Spirit to inspire you so that as you write your letter in gratitude that you are able to recall the specific things that God has done in your life.

When you have finished writing the letter, read it. Perhaps read it two or three times. Then, just as you have done with passages of Sacred Scripture, ask yourself what word or phrase is speaking to you from your letter to God.

What words stood out to you as you prayed?
What did you find stirring in your heart?

More

"Mary of Magdala came to the tomb early in the morning, while it was still dark, and saw the stone removed from the tomb."

– JOHN 20:1, NAB

Easter Sunday

Imagine the wait. The Blessed Mother waited. John waited. Mary Magdalene waited. The pain of separation from Jesus would have been as intense as the joys of their friendship with him. They loved him enough to endure the eyewitness of his torture and death.

Because of that love, the wait in the darkness is tumultuous.

Shattered, sober, and silent, Mary Magdalene went "early in the morning, while it was still dark, and saw the stone removed from the tomb." Imagine her panic. The only thing worse than having her Lord crucified is having his body stolen and desecrated. Mary Magdalene peers into the tomb, hoping that his body is still there. But something is different here, for she realizes he has risen!

Mary Magdalene is filled with joy! When she first knew Jesus, she was searching and bound in her sin. But through the years of their friendship, Mary Magdalene has tasted the freedom and the abundant life he has promised all those who know and love him. She knows she is made for more.

Go back to the early days of the journey. Why have we been on this journey? Why did Jesus come? Why Lent? Why were we walking together? Jesus came "so that they might have life and have it more abundantly" (John 10:10, NAB). Jesus came because there is more. You have changed. You are different. You cannot go back to who you were before Lent started. You are made for more.

For Your Prayer

Rise very early—before sunrise—and wait in the darkness. Sit in the darkness and wait. As the sun rises, thank God for his love. Give thanks to the risen Lord, who died and rose for you!

What words stood out to you as you prayed?
What did you find stirring in your heart?

_____

_____

_____

_____

_____

_____

_____

_____

_____

_____

_____

_____

_____

_____

"He is not here, he has been raised just as he said."

– MATTHEW 28:6

Notes

1. Benedict XVI, *Deus Caritas Est* (December 25, 2005), 1.

2. Benedict XVI, *Jesus of Nazareth: From the Baptism in the Jordan to the Transfiguration*, trans. Adrian J. Walker (New York: Doubleday, 2007), 29.

3. Ignatius, Fourteenth Rule, in Timothy Gallagher, *The Discernment of Spirits: An Ignatian Guide for Everyday Living* (New York: Crossroad, 2005), Kindle edition (under "The Text of the Rules").

4. Ignatius, Twelfth Rule, in Gallagher.

5. Ignatius, Fourth Rule, in Gallagher.

6. Ignatius, Seventh Rule, in Gallagher.

7. Benedict XVI, *Deus Caritas Est*, 1.

8. James Keating, "The Eucharist and the Healing of Affection for Sin," *Emmanuel* (March–April 2007), available at priestlyformation.org.

9. Paul VI, *Evangelii Nuntiandi* (December 8, 1975), 41.

10. Francis, *Misericordia et Misera* (November 20, 2016), 2.

11. Benedict XVI, *Deus Caritas Est*, 18.

12. Keating, "The Eucharist and the Healing of Affection for Sin."

13. Keating.

Credits

Executive Producer

Jonathan Strate

General Manager

Jeffrey Cole

Product Manager and Content Manager

Julia Coppa Bernetsky

Project Manager

Alexa Smith

Art

Mike Moyers

Editorial

Rebecca Robinson, Julia Coppa Bernetsky

Graphics

Sarah Stueve, Stella Ziegler

Video

Matt Pirrall, Coronation Studios

Marketing

Mark Leopold, Julia Amting